The Architecture
of the
ARM Microprocessors

a Resource Guide

Patrick H. Stakem

© 2011, 2015

3rd edition, 7th in Computer Architecture series

ISBN - 9781520215846

Introduction

The ARM processor has come a long way from being an obscure British microprocessor of the 1980's to being the dominant basis for the current generation of smart phones, and tablet computers. They are also used extensively in television set-top boxes, routers, and embedded applications. The ARM architecture parts still represent the highest volume of 32-bit processors being shipped, as of this writing.

In 2010, over 6 billion ARM chips were sold, mostly into the smartphone market. ARM is the target architecture for the GNU/linux-based Android operating system, and the ARM has ports of OpenSolaris, FreeBSD, OpenBSD, NetBSD, and various GNU/linux variations, including Gentoo, Debian, Slackware, and Ubuntu, among others.

In 1983, the British company Acorn Computers Ltd. was shopping for a new 16-bit processor to replace the 8-bit Mostek 6502 that they were then using. Some say that Acorn was rejected by Intel, others say that Acorn didn't like either the Intel 80286 or the Motorola MC 68000. In any case, the company decided to develop its own processor called the Acorn RISC Machine, or ARM. The company had been started in Cambridge, UK, in 1978. The name *Acorn* was supposed to suggest expandability and growth. The company had development samples, known as the ARM1, by 1985; production models (ARM2) were ready the following year. The original ARM chip contained 30,000 transistors. Acorn Computers was taken over by Olivetti in 1985 and renamed Element 14, LTD, in 1999 (element number 14 is silicon). That company was in turn taken over by Broadcom in the year 2000.

The ARM started out as destined for the desktop, but along the way, got diverted mostly to embedded use. Now, more powerful ARM chips are beginning to challenge the pc and server markets, currently owned by the Intel architecture.

ARM is an Instruction Set Architecture (ISA) specification. It is instantiated in silicon by numerous companies under license. ARM Holdings PLC, a British Multinational company, is the inheritor of the intellectual property (IP) of the 32-bit CPU design, and licenses its use worldwide. The products include the licensable intellectual property for the ARM7, ARM9, ARM11, and the Cortex series. Derivative products include the StrongARM, the Freescale series, the Xscale, the Snapdragon, Samsung's Hummingbird, the A4 and A5 by Apple, and Texas Instruments products incorporating digital signal processing functionality, among others. This is similar to the situation with Intel's ISA-32, with chips of that architecture built by Intel, and chips with a different implementation of the architecture built by AMD and others. The Intel ISA-16 and ISA-32 addressed the desktop and server market, but embedded versions were also available.

The computers built from the ARM CPU chips were popular in the UK, but not a big hit worldwide. They included the BBC Micro, and the Archimedes. The BBC machine was dominant for a while in the educational market in the UK. Acorn Computers has been referred to as the "Apple" of the UK.

The ARM architecture today accounts for more than 75% of all 32-bit embedded processors. Hundreds of millions are in cellular phones and tablets. The ARM architecture provides a simple and standard platform for embedded systems. Embedded systems differ in their architecture and requirements from desktop and server architectures. The problem domains have different requirements. Where the Intel x86 architecture came to dominate the desktop and server areas, the ARM architecture is dominating the small embedded market. A hardware architecture definition is necessary, but it must be accompanied by an equally good software architecture. This is just as true for the ARM. Code can be developed in Java or variants of the most languages and many off-the-shelf operating systems are available. The ARM architecture reached critical mass in the embedded market niche. ARM separates the Intellectual Property of the design and the Instruction Set Architecture from the implementation. The ARM architecture has at this point more than 700 licenses, and it grows by 100 per year.

The author assumes a certain level of familiarization with computer architecture for the reader. Details are provided in appendices, and a rich set of references are included. ARM implementations are very dynamic, and many new features are evolving as the technology permits. You use and touch many ARM processors every day, although they are not necessarily obvious.

The author uses the ARM processor as the basis for his Embedded Microprocessor Systems course in the Engineering for Professional Program (EPP) at the Johns Hopkins University. He has used embedded ARM processors in NASA Robotics projects, involving large autonomous Earth Rovers; essentially, satellites at a very low altitude.

The Advanced RISC Machine

ARM claims the distinction of having the first commercial reduced instruction set computer (RISC) microprocessor, circa 1985. It was not well known in the US. ARM processors represent a non-traditional RISC design, optimized for low power consumption. The chip's high power efficiency gave it an edge in battery powered portable equipment. ARM currently has one of the best MIPS per watt ratings in the industry.

The ARM RISC processor project was started by Acorn computers of Cambridge, England in 1983. The current ARM line started with a design effort by Advanced RISC Machine, Ltd. a company that licensed designs for fabrication. The actual fabrication of the devices has been done by VLSI, Plessey, Sharp, Intel, and many others. The major applications for the device are in 32-bit embedded control, and the portable computing market, including Apple's 'Newton' palmtop product. The ARM was also used in the Teenage Mutant Ninja Turtle animated puppets. *ARM* describes architecture, and a family of processors, 32 bits in word size. There are only 10 basic instruction types. On-chip is set of 16 registers, a barrel shifter, and hardware multiplier. According to the designers, the ARM was easier to program in assembly language than most other RISC processors. The ARM was designed as a static device, meaning that the clock may be arbitrarily slowed or stopped, with no loss of internal state. This also affects power consumption, which was specified at 1.5 mA per Mhz for the processor core, one of the lowest in the industry. The ARM is also available as an ASIC macrocell, allowing integration into systems at the chip level. The ARM6 core had 37k transistors. The low-end member of the family, the ARM2 (86C010) implemented the core, with no cache or memory management unit (MMU). The ARM3 (86C020) included the core plus a 4-kilobyte unified cache, a coprocessor interface, and semaphore support for multiprocessing. The ARM600 (86C600) added an MMU (memory management unit) and a write buffer. Other members of the family included the 86C060, and the 26-bit bus 86C061 version, that provided compatibility with earlier products, and the ARM 610.

The ARM2 had a 32-bit data bus with a 26-bit address space. It implemented twenty-seven 32-bit registers. The program counter was 24 bits. The design was simple and streamlined; being implemented in 30,000 transistors, half the count of Motorola's contemporary 68000 chip.

Acorn had design experience with RISC designs going back to 1983, and marketed their RISC-based Archimedes computers in Europe by 1987. Originally a dynamic logic design for minimal silicon area, the complexities of this approach convinced the designers that the core should be fully static. An asynchronous ARM design exists.

The ARM 6 model (v3 architecture) resulted from a collaboration of Acorn's chip design team with Apple Computer and VLSI Technology. The chip was released in 1992, and became the basis for Apple's Newton PDA, among other devices.

The next generation ARM7 was produced in silicon by early 1994. It had a faster multiplier unit, and could operate at lower voltages. In 0.8 micron CMOS, operation at 33 MHz was possible. Models with enhanced debug capabilities were also available. Texas Instruments implemented the ARM core in their TMS370 processor line, and augmented the architecture with digital signal processing extensions.

Architecture of the Legacy ARMs

The architecture of the ARM600 processor was driven in part by Apple's requirements. It had a 32-bit address bus, and supported virtual memory. The hardware was optimized for applications that are both price and power sensitive. The processor supported both a user and a supervisor mode. Not a Harvard design, the ARM caches data and instructions together on-chip. However, it has a 64-way set associative cache with 256 lines of 4 words each. The cache was virtual, and the MMU (memory management unit) must be enabled for caching to become effective. A settable bit allows the I/O space to be marked as not-cachable. The chip's heritage in RISC and embedded applications give it a fast interrupt response and good code density. It had a small die size, leading to both low power consumption and low cost of production. A fully static design allows a slow-down or power-down with no loss of state. This is a critical factor in battery-powered equipment.

The architecture is load/store with no memory reference instructions. The load/store operand is a register (32-bit) or an immediate constant. These operations may specify operand increment or decrement, pre- or post-operation. There is a load/store- multiple feature, essentially a block data transfer, but it affects interrupt response, because it is not interuptable. A three-operand format is used. The hardware includes a barrel shifter that one operand always goes through. A barrel shifter is a combinatorial circuit that takes no clock cycles for its operation. The instruction execution process used a 3-stage pipeline. A Booth algorithm hardware multiplier was used.

Multiply and multiply/accumulate (MAC) take up to 16 cycles. Although the instruction encoding only allows 16 registers to be used for addresses, the instruction format allows for a complete orthogonal encoding of ALU operations. An integer multiply/accumulate instruction is included. The instruction encoding, which is very "microcode" like, gives a very large number of possible instruction cases, given the conditional execution feature. Floating point operations are not supported in the core, nor is out-of-order execution. The processor provided a complete generic coprocessor interface for up to 16 devices. A floating point coprocessor was designed by ARM Ltd, and built by Plessey.

The chip uses a Von Neumann architecture, with only 1 address space. Data path width is 32-bits for data, with a 26-bit address on the 610 and earlier processors, expanding to a 32-bit address on the 620 and subsequent. A write buffer is included, with space for two pending writes of up to 8 words. When used with the write-thru cache, this feature allows the processor to avoid waiting for external memory writes to complete.

Reset initialization provides for the execution of NOP's when activated, and going to the reset vector address when deactivated. The 610 used a maximum 12 MHz clock, going to 20 MHz on the 620. JTAG debugging support was provided in the ARM600 and ARM610. Request lines for two interrupts were included. The ARM60 was a CMOS Macrocell, available as a VHDL model.

Several support chips for the ARM family processors were available. These included the 410 I/O controller, the 110 memory controller, and the 310 video controller. The 110 memory controller provided control signals for DRAM, DMA arbitration, and MMU functions. Three levels of protection were provided to regions of supervisor, operating system and user. In later versions of ARM, as more functionality could be included in the silicon, these features migrated onto the CPU chip.

Support for slow ROM was also provided. Up to 4 megabytes of DRAM could be controlled by the chip. For the memory mapping, a default page size of 4 kilobytes was used, but this could be changed to 8, 16, or 32 bits under programming control. Multiple memory controller units could be used in a system.

The 310 video controller accessed video ram, and outputted data through a color look-up table to a CRT device. It included three 40-bit DAC's, and could serialize to 8 bits per pixel. It also included stereo sound generation capability.

The architecture of the 86C410 I/O controller is interesting. This device included four timers, an interrupt controller, a clock generator, a serial port, and 6 programmable I/O pins. With the processor, this peripheral forms the basis for many embedded control applications. The support chip was compatible with all members of the processor family. Two of the timers could function as baud rate generators for serial communications. There was a bi-directional serial keyboard interface, interrupt mask, request, and status for the two interrupt lines of the processor, with 14 level and two edge triggered interrupts. This device provided interface for a variety of external peripherals to the ARM. Now, with the ability to produce more complex chips, all this functionality is commonly included on the CPU.

The complete ARM600 chip drew 5 mA per MHz, or about 1/2 watt operating at 5 volts and 20 MHz The ARM610 was available in 84-pin or a 144-pin package. The 620 model used a 160-pin package.

All ARM instructions of the ten basic types are 32 bits in size. An interesting feature is that all instructions are conditionally executable - not just the branches! This means that the programmer does not need to conditionally branch over instructions - the instruction itself is conditional. This feature is under program control via setting of the S-bit. Conditions for execution include the cases always and never. Instructions have 3 operand references, 2 source and 1 destination. Integer math operations include add, subtract, and multiply. No floating point instructions were provided in the baseline architecture. Load/Store operations provide memory access, and a block transfer is provided, that can be aborted. There are AND and XOR logical operations, as well as bit clears and compares. Flow control is accomplished by branch, and branch and link. A software interrupt mechanism provides for supervisor service calls.

The ARM architecture provided visibility and use of the twenty-seven 32-bit registers. The ARM620 had 37 32-bit registers in 6 overlapping sets, and 6 modes of operation. Sixteen registers were visible to the user, the rest being reserved for internal uses, such as the program counter. The state of the general purpose registers at reset time is unknown. Although the registers are general purpose, register 15 is the program counter. This has some advantages and disadvantages. If we use R15 as the destination of an ALU operation, we get a type of indirect branch for free. However, this approach doesn't support delayed branches, which require two program counters for a short while.

Register 14 holds the return address for calls, and is shadowed in all cases. The stack pointer is generally held in Register 13, with Register 12 being used for stack frame pointer. The stack pointer points to the last stacked item. With each stack push operation, the SP is decremented, and the item is put on the stack. Interrupts and the supervisor mode have private stack pointers and link registers.

In terms of byte ordering, the 610 was little-endian, but the 620 could operate in little- or big- endian mode. Supported data types included bytes and 32-bit words. Development support included an ANSI c compiler and run-time libraries, an assembler with linker and librarian, a floating point emulator package, symbolic debugger, and instruction set emulator. Third-party offerings included compilers for Fortran-77, Pascal, LISP, and Modula-2, and a RTX real-time kernel, from ATI Corp. Hardware evaluation and prototyping cards were available for the pc bus, and as a platform- independent, stand-alone unit. A bootstrap rom code and resident debug monitor was available, with a machine level debugger. Host environments include the pc and Sun. A floating point coprocessor was available to support IEEE floating point operations.

The cache was a 4-kbyte unified organization in the ARM620. It was a 64-way set associative unit, with a line size of 16 bytes. Semaphores provided multiprocessor support. Write-through policy was used. Memory could be marked as not cachable in control register 3, allowing for the memory mapped I/O region. MMU support was provided on the ARM610. The ARM architecture implements facilities for object- oriented programming, including memory protection strategies, and features for real-time concurrent garbage collection. The MMU controls memory access permissions, with tables in main memory, and a 32 element translation lookaside buffer on chip. Pages can be 1 megabyte, 4 or 64 kilobytes in size. Access permissions are mapped separately and manipulated independently of addresses. Address faults are handled separately from permission faults. Semaphore operations for multiprocessing are implemented by means of indivisible read-lock-write bus cycles. There are two levels of access permission maintained. The first is straightforward, but the domain level is a differentiator for the ARM MMU. Domain access, maintained in a register, is defined as the four cases: no access, client, reserved, or manager. For the 'client' case, access permission checking is traditional and straightforward. For the manager case, an override of the encoded permission allows unrestricted access to the section. This facilitated the task of a garbage collector. The domain concept allows the privilege bits in the access control register to override both levels of protection encoded in the descriptor fields. Access to the control register is necessarily a restricted operation.

There are two interrupts, regular and fast, with two corresponding modes. In fast mode, there is a 2.5 clock interrupt latency best case. Exception vectors are used. A software interrupt instruction is included, and execution of an undefined or unsupported instruction causes an exception (abort mode) that may be used for software emulation. Exceptions can also occur due to internal events, such as undefined instruction. An abort pin provides the MMU with a signal to the processor to indicate a memory access problem. Worst case latency in the fast interrupt case is 25 cycles.

ARM Classic

The ARM Classic processors include the implementations of ARM architecture versions 4, 5, and 6. With these models, ARM proved itself in the marketplace. Probably close to 20 billion ARM Classic units were shipped. ARM Classic units ARM7, 9, and 11, are still used, with an estimated 220 partners producing product in 2010. The ARM architecture still represents the highest number of 32-bit processors shipped.

V4

The StrongARM was a family of microprocessors that implemented the ARM V4 instruction set architecture (ISA). It was developed by Digital Equipment Corporation (DEC) and later sold to Intel, who continued to manufacture it before replacing it with the XScale series.

The StrongARM was a collaborative project between DEC and Advanced RISC Machines to create a faster ARM. The StrongARM was designed to address the upper-end of the low-power embedded market, where users needed more performance than the standard ARM could deliver. Targets were devices such as the emerging personal digital assistants and set-top boxes.

In order to tap the design talent of Silicon Valley, DEC opened a new design center in Palo Alto. The design center, led by Computer Architect Dan Dobberpuhl, was the main design site for the StrongARM project. The project was initiated in 1995, and quickly delivered their first design, the SA-110.

When the semiconductor division of DEC was sold to Intel, many engineers from the Palo Alto design group moved to SiByte, a start-up company then designing MIPS-based system-on-a-chips (SoCs) for the networking market. The Austin design group spun off to become Alchemy Semiconductor, another start-up company designing MIPS SoCs for the hand-held market. A new StrongARM core was developed by Intel and introduced in 2000 as the XScale.

The SA-110 was the first microprocessor in the StrongARM family. The first versions, operating up to 200 MHz were announced in 1996. Volume production was achieved in mid-1996 with faster versions (266 MHz) announced. Throughout that year, the SA-110 was the highest performance embedded microprocessor available for portable devices. The SA-110's first design win was the Apple MessagePad 2000. It was also used in the Acorn Computers RISC PC.

The SA-110 had a very simple microarchitecture. It was a scalar design that executed instructions in-order with a five-stage classic RISC pipeline. The microprocessor was partitioned into several blocks. The IBOX contained hardware that operated in the first two stages of the pipeline such as the program counter. It fetched, decoded and issued instructions. Instruction fetch occurs during the first stage, decode and issue during the second. The IBOX decodes the more complex instructions in the ARM instruction set by translating them dynamically into sequences of simpler instructions. The IBOX also handled branch instructions. The SA-110 did not have branch prediction hardware, but had other branch acceleration mechanisms.

Instruction execution started at stage three. The hardware that operated during this stage was contained in the EBOX, which comprised the register file, arithmetic logic unit (ALU), barrel shifter, multiplier and condition code logic. The register file had three read ports and two write ports. The ALU and barrel shifter executed instructions in a single cycle. The multiplier was not pipelined and had a latency of multiple cycles.

The IMMU and DMMU were memory management units for instructions and data, respectively. Each MMU contained a 32-entry fully associative translation lookaside buffer (TLB) that could map 4 KB, 64 KB or 1 MB pages. The write buffer (WB) had eight 16-byte entries. It enabled the pipelining of store operations. The bus interface unit (BIU) provided the SA-110 with an external interface. The PLL generated the internal clock signal from an external 3.68 MHz clock signal.

The instruction cache and data cache each had a capacity of 16 KB and were 32-way set-associative and virtually addressed. The SA-110 was designed to be used with slow (low-cost) memory and therefore the high set associativity allowed a higher hit rate, and the use of virtual addresses allowed memory to be simultaneously cached and uncached. The caches took up half the die area.

The SA-110 contained 2.5 million transistors and was fabricated by DEC in its proprietary CMOS-6 process in Hudson, Massachusetts. It used a power supply with a variable voltage of 1.2 to 2.2 volts (V) to enable designs to have a balance between power consumption and performance (higher voltages allow higher clock rates). The SA-110 was packaged in a 144-pin thin quad flat pack (TQFP).

The SA-1100 was a derivative of the SA-110 developed by DEC. Announced in 1997, the SA-1100 was targeted to portable applications such as PDAs. The data cache was reduced in size to 8 KB to allow implementation of features for this application.

The new features included integrated memory, PCMCIA, and color LCD controllers connected to an on-die system bus, and five serial I/O channels that are connected to a peripheral bus attached to the system bus. The memory controller supported a variety of memory technologies. A PCMCIA controller was included. The memory address and data bus were shared with the PCMCIA interface. The serial I/O channels implemented a slave USB interface, a SDLC, two UARTs, an IrDA interface, and a synchronous serial port.

The SA-1100 had a companion chip, the SA-1101. It provided additional peripherals to complement those integrated on the SA-1100 such as a video output port, two PS/2 ports, a USB controller and a PCMCIA controller that replaced the earlier one. The SA-1100 contained 2.5 million transistors.

The SA-1110 was a derivative of the SA-110. Intel had discontinued the SA-1110 in early 2003. The SA-1110 was available in 133 or 206 MHz versions. It differed from the SA-1100 by featuring support for 66 MHz (133 MHz version) or 103 MHz (206 MHz version) Synchronous dynamic random access memory (SDRAM). Its companion chip, which provided additional support for peripherals, was the SA-1111. The SA-1110 was packaged in a

256-pin micro ball grid array (BGA). It was used in mobile phones, personal data assistants (PDAs) such as the Compaq iPAQ and HP Jornada, and the Sharp SL-5x00 GNU/linux Based Platforms.

The SA-1500 was a derivative of the SA-110 developed by DEC initially targeted for set-top boxes. It was designed and manufactured in low volumes by DEC but was never put into production by Intel. The SA-1500 was available at speeds of 200 to 300 MHz. The SA-1500 featured an enhanced SA-110 core, an on-chip coprocessor called the Attached Media Processor (AMP), and an on-chip SDRAM and I/O bus controller. The SDRAM controller supported 100 MHz SDRAM, and the I/O controller implemented a 32-bit I/O bus that may run at frequencies up to 50 MHz for connecting to peripherals and the SA-1501 companion chip.

The AMP implemented a long instruction word instruction set containing instructions specifically designed for multimedia, such as integer and floating-point multiply–accumulate and SIMD arithmetic. Each long instruction word was 64-bits wide and specified an arithmetic operation and a branch or a load/store. Instructions operated on operands from a 64-entry 36-bit register file or on a set of control registers. The AMP communicated with the SA-110 core via an on-chip bus and it shared the data cache with the SA-110. The AMP contained an ALU with a shifter, a branch unit, a load/store unit, a multiply–accumulate unit, and a single-precision floating-point unit. The AMP also supported user-defined instructions via a 512-entry writable control store.

The SA-1501 companion chip provided additional video and audio processing capabilities and various I/O functions such as PS/2 ports, and a parallel port. The SA-1500 contained 3.3 million transistors.

The ARM v7 architecture includes hardware debugging features such as breakpoints and a debug mode. ARM-7 architecture has been implemented in a variety of cores. ARM-7 introduced the Thumb 16-bit instruction set providing improved code density. The most widely used ARM7 designs implement the ARMv4T architecture. These use a Von Neumann approach, the few versions supporting a cache do not separate data and instruction

15

caches. The Thumb state is indicated by the status of a bit in the execution program status register.

One historically significant model, the ARM7DI is notable for having introduced JTAG based on-chip debugging; the preceding ARM6 cores did not support it. The "D" represented a JTAG TAP for debugging; the "I" denoted an ICEBreaker debug module supporting hardware breakpoints and watchpoints, and a feature for stalling the system for debugging.

The ARM7-TDMI (ARM7-Thumb+Debug+Multiplier+ICE) processor was a 32-bit RISC CPU designed by ARM, and licensed for manufacture by numerous semiconductor companies. As of 2009, it remained one of the most widely used ARM cores, and could be found in numerous deeply embedded system designs. The ARM7TDMI-S variant was the synthesizable core.

It was intended for mobile devices and other low power electronics. This processor architecture was capable of up to 130 MIPS. The ARM7TDMI processor core implemented ARM Architecture v4T. The processor supported both 32-bit and 16-bit instructions via the ARM and Thumb instruction sets.

Jazelle

Jazelle refers to a technique called direct bytecode execution (DBX) which allows the processor to execute Java byte code in hardware. This is like having a third execution state which implements JAVA direct-execute machine along with the native ARM and Thumb modes. Between the fetch and decode stages of the instruction pipeline, an inserted stage allows selected bytecodes to be converted into strings of native ARM instructions. This transfers interpretation of Java byte codes into hardware for the most common and simple codes. The others follow the path to the software Java Virtual Machine. There is an application binary interface (ABI) maintained by ARM Holdings for this. The current program status register (cpsr) has a "J" bit to indicate Jazelle state. The complication comes in giving register access to the Java bytecodes. The Jazelle scheme has been mostly replaced by the Thumb execution environment (ThumbEE) found on Cortex -A8 and -A9.

Thumb

The Thumb Instruction set state is an extension to the ARM 7 architecture. This is a 16-bit subset of the ARM instruction set. This reduces functionality but provides a greater code density. Sections of code that are computer-intensive can be hand-optimized for the Thumb mode. The Nintendo Game Boy Advance unit used this. The Thumb architecture has been extended to ARM9.

To improve compiled code-density, processors since the ARM7TDMI have featured the Thumb instruction set state. In this state, the processor executes the Thumb instruction set. Most of the Thumb instructions directly map to normal ARM instructions. The memory savings comes from making some of the operands implicit, and limiting the number of options compared to the standard ARM instructions executed in the ARM instruction set state.

In Thumb, the 16-bit opcodes have less functionality. Only branches can be conditional, and many opcodes are restricted to accessing only half of the CPU's general purpose registers. The shorter opcodes give improved code density overall, even though some operations require extra instructions. In situations where the memory port or bus width is constrained to less than 32 bits, the shorter Thumb opcodes allow increased performance compared with 32-bit ARM code, as less program code needs to be loaded into the processor using the limited memory bandwidth.

Embedded hardware in the Game Boy Advance unit had a small amount of RAM accessible with a full 32-bit datapath. A typical approach was to compile Thumb code and hand-optimize the most CPU-intensive sections with full 32-bit ARM instructions.

The first processor with a Thumb instruction decoder was the ARM7TDMI. All ARM9 and later families, including XScale, have included the Thumb instruction decoder.

Thumb-2 technology made its debut in 2003. Thumb-2 extended the limited 16-bit instruction set of Thumb with additional 32-bit instructions to give the instruction set more latitude, producing a variable-length instruction set. A goal of Thumb-2 was to achieve code density similar to Thumb (16-bit) with performance similar to the ARM instruction set on 32-bit memory.

The ARM-7 architecture was used in the Apple iPod, Lego Mindstorms NXT, various Nokia mobile phones, the Nintendo DS and Game Boy Advance, the Roomba 500 series floor cleaning robot from iRobot, Sirius Satellite Radio receivers, and many others.

V5

The XScale microprocessor core is Intel's and Marvell's implementation of the ARMv5 architecture, and consists of several distinct families. The XScale Application Processors include the I/O Processors (IOP); the Network Processors (IXP); the Control Plane Processors (IXC); and the Consumer Electronics Processors (CE). The XScale effort at Intel was started after the purchase of DEC's StrongARM division in 1998.

In June 2006, Intel sold the XScale PXA business to Marvell Technology Group. This allowed Intel to focus its resources on its core x86 architecture and server businesses. Marvell holds a full Architecture License for ARM, allowing it to design chips to implement the ARM instruction set. Intel continued manufacturing XScale processors for Marvell. The IXP and IOP processors were not part of the deal. Intel continues to hold an ARM license as well.

The XScale architecture was based on the ARMv5TE ISA but without the floating point instructions. XScale uses a seven-stage integer and an eight-stage memory superpipelined microarchitecture.

All the generations of XScale are 32-bit ARMv5TE processors. They have a 32 kB data cache and a 32 kB instruction cache. First and second generation XScale cores also have a 2 kB mini-data cache. Products of 3rd generation XScale have up to 512 kB unified L2 cache.

Standalone processors such as the 80200 and 80219 were targeted primarily to PCI applications. The PXA210 was Intel's entry-level XScale product, targeted at cellphone applications.

Multimedia extensions (MMX) features for Xscale were also implemented as 43 new SIMD instructions containing the full MMX instruction set and the integer instructions from Intel's x86 SSE instruction set. This represents Intel's major contribution to the ARM. MMX also included new instructions unique to XScale. MMX provided 16 additional 64-bit registers that are treated as an array of two 32-bit words, four 16-bit half-words or eight 8-bit bytes. The XScale core can perform up to eight adds or four MACs in parallel in a single cycle. This capability was used to enhance speed in decoding and encoding of multimedia data and in game support. An internal 256 kB SRAM was included to reduce power consumption and latency due to off-chip memory.

The Marvell PXA16x was targeted to cost-sensitive consumer products such as digital picture frames, E-Readers, multifunction printer user interface (UI) displays, interactive VoIP phones, IP surveillance cameras, and home control gadgets.

The PXA930 and PXA935 processor series were built using an architecture developed by Marvell called the Sheeva core. This supported the ARMv5TE, ARMv6 and ARMv7 instruction sets. This new architecture was a significant leap forward. The PXA930 was used in the Blackberry Bold 9700.

The IOP line of processors was designed to allow computers and storage devices to transfer data and increase performance by offloading I/O functionality from the main CPU of the device. The IOP3XX processors were based on the XScale architecture and designed to replace the older Intel 80219 I/O processor and i960 family of chips. There were ten different IOP processors available. Clock speeds ranged from 100 MHz to 1.2 GHz. The processors differed in PCI bus type and speed, memory type, maximum memory allowable, and the number of processor cores.

The XScale core is utilized in the second generation of Intel's IXP network processor line, while the first generation used StrongARM cores.

XScale microprocessors were used in products such as the RIM BlackBerry handheld, the Dell Axim family of Pocket PCs, most of the Zire, Treo and Tungsten Handheld lines by Palm, later versions of the Sharp Zaurus, the Motorola A780, the Acer n50, the Compaq iPaq 3900 series and many other PDAs. It was also used as the main CPU in several desktop computers running RISC OS and GNU/linux. The XScale is also found in the Amazon Kindle E-Book reader. The XScale IOP33x Storage I/O processors are used in Intel Xeon-based server platforms.

With the ARM-9 generation, ARM moved from a von Neumann architecture to a Harvard architecture with separate instruction and data buses (and caches), for increasing potential speed. Most silicon chips integrating these cores will package them as a modified Harvard architecture, combining the two address buses on the other side of separated CPU caches and tightly coupled memories. ARM9 introduced DSP extensions, Jazelle support, and floating point support.

Switching to a Harvard architecture entailed implementing a non-unified cache, so that instruction fetches do not impact data reads and writes and vice versa. ARM9 cores have separate data and address bus signals, which chip designers can use in various ways. In most cases they connect at least part of the address space in von Neumann style, used for both instructions and data.

ARM9E and ARM9EJ implement longer pipelines. The ARMv5TE architecture includes some DSP-like instruction set extensions supporting 8-, 16- and 32- bit instruction sets.

V6

The ARM11 introduced the ARMv6 architectural additions. These include SIMD media instructions, multiprocessor support and a new cache architecture. They include an improved pipeline compared to previous ARM9 or ARM10 families. The ARM9 was used in smartphones from Apple, Nokia, and others. The initial ARM11 core was released to licensees in late 2002. Version 6 introduced Jazelle.

There are Thumb2-only (no ARM instructions) ARMv6-M cores (Cortex-M0 and Cortex-M1), addressing microcontroller applications; ARM11 cores target more demanding applications. The ARM11 extends the ARM9. It incorporates all ARM926EJ-S features and adds the ARMv6 instructions for media support (SIMD) and accelerated interrupt response.

Microarchitecture improvements in ARM11 cores include SIMD instructions which can double MPEG-4 and audio digital signal processing algorithm speed. The cache is physically addressed, solving cache aliasing problems and reducing context switch overhead. Unaligned and mixed-endian data access is supported. There is an improved pipeline, supporting faster clock speeds (up to 1 GHz), and the pipeline is now 8 stages versus 5. Out-of-order completion of instructions is supported, as is dynamic branch prediction/folding. Cache misses are not allowed to block execution of non-dependent instructions. Load/Store parallelism is provided as are 64-bit data paths. All of these features provide performance at the cost of complexity.

Thumb-2 extended both the ARM and Thumb instruction set with additional instructions, including bit-field manipulation, table branches, and conditional execution. A new "Unified Assembly Language" (UAL) supports generation of either Thumb-2 or ARM instructions from the same source code. Versions of Thumb seen on ARMv7 processors are as capable as native ARM code. This required the use of a new "IT" (if-then) instruction, which permits up to four successive instructions to execute based on a tested condition. When compiling into ARM code, this can be ignored, but when compiling into Thumb-2, it generates an actual instruction.

The TrustZone security extensions were introduced with the ARMv6. This approach to security involves dual cores and hardware-based access control. The cores host two execution states at different levels of trust. OpenVirtualization is the Open source version of the TrustZone.

ARM11 supports the ARM, Thumb, and Thumb-2 ISA's, and includes DSP and SIMD extensions. It includes Jazelle, floating point, TrustZone, and cache. ARM11-based chips are available from Freescale, Nvidia, PLX

21

Technology, Qualcomm Samsung, Texas Instruments and others. The TI OMAP2 series has a TMS320 C55x or C64x DSP as a second core. The ARM-11 can be found in the Apple iPhone and iPod Touch, the Amazon Kindle e-book reader, the Nintendo 3DS, numerous cellphones, the Nokia N800 Internet Tablet, and some digital picture frames.

ARM Cortex

The ARM Cortex processors are the latest in the 32-bit series, and extend into multicore and 64-bit models for higher performance. There are three basic models of the Cortex processors, targeting different applications areas. These are provided as licensable products by ARM, Ltd., and produced by multiple chip manufacturers.

Cortex-A

Cortex-A processors are targeted to the smartphone and mobile computing markets, as well as digital television, set-top boxes, and printers.

The Cortex-A5 optionally supports floating point and NEON media processing. The memory management was improved, and virtual memory is supported. The design is targeted to energy efficiency. Voltages are 1.0 or 1.1 volts, with clock speeds to 1 GHz. Up to 4 cores are supported. Instruction and data L1 caches can extend to 64k each.

NEON implements an advanced SIMD instruction set and was first introduced with the ARM Cortex –A8 model. This is an extension of the FPU with a quad Multiply-and-Accumulate (MAC) unit and additional 64-bit and 128-bit registers.

Single instruction, multiple data (SIMD) describes computers with multiple processing elements that perform the same operation on multiple data simultaneously. Thus, such machines exploit data level parallelism. Vector processing is where a single operation is applied to a 1-dimensional array of data.

The Cortex-A8 is a superscalar architecture, with dual instruction issue. The NEON SIMD unit is optional, as is floating point support. The architecture supports Thumb-2 and Jazelle, but only single core. Advanced branch prediction algorithms provide an accuracy rate reportedly approaching 95%. Up to a four megabyte Level-2 cache is provided. There is a 128-bit SIMD engine. Cortex A-8 chips have been implemented by Samsung, TI, and Freescale, among others.

The Samsung Hummingbird is a system-on-a-chip based on the Cortex A8, and including a GPU. These parts are used in Samsung's Galaxy line of tablets. The Qualcomm Snapdragon chip is based on the Cortex-A8 with the ARM7 instruction set, and includes a GPU. The chip is used in smartphones, tablets, and smartbooks. The Snapdragon is produced in dual and quad-core models.

The Cortex-A9 can have multiple cores that are multi-issue superscalar and support out-of-order and speculative execution using register renaming. It has an 8-stage pipeline. Two instructions per cycle can be decoded. There are up to 64k of 4-way set associative Level-1 cache, with up to 512k of Level 2. A 64-bit Harvard architecture memory access allows for maximum bandwidth. Four doubleword writes take five machine cycles. Floating point units and a media processing engine are available for each core. The Cortex-A supports the Thumb-2 instructions.

The Cortex-A9 is implemented in a series of system-on-a-chip devices from multiple manufacturers. As an example, the STMElectronics SPEAr1310 is a dual-core Cortex-A SMP. It has dual cores, and can support either symmetric or asymmetric multiprocessing. It has a 32k instruction and a 32k data cache at Level 1. The Level 2 cache is unified, and is 512k bytes in size. The on-chip interprocessor bus is 64 bits wide. The chip includes 32k of bootrom and 32k of SRAM, with support for external NAND or NOR flash and static ram.

The Cortex chip includes dual Gigabit ports, three fast Ethernet, three PCIe links, three SATA ports, dual USB-2, dual CAN bus, dual HDLC controllers, dual I^{2}C ports, and six UARTs operating up to 5 Megabaud. There is an integrated LCD controller with touchscreen support, a keyboard controller, and a memory card interface. It supports thirteen timers and a real time clock, in addition to a cryptographic accelerator. Included are dual 8-channel DMA controllers, a JPEG codec in hardware, and 8-input, 10-bit A/D, and JTAG support.

The Cortex-A15 is multicore, and has an out-of-order superscalar pipeline. The chip was introduced in 2012, and is available from TI, NVidia, Samsung, and others. It can address a terabyte of memory. The integer pipeline is 15 stages long, and the floating point pipeline is up to 25 stages. The instruction issue is speculative. There can be 4 cores per cluster, two clusters per chip. Each core has separate 32k data and instruction caches. The level-2 cache controller supports up to 4 megabytes per cluster. DSP and NEON SIMD are supported, as is floating point. Hardware virtualization support is included. Both Thumb-2 and Jazelle modes are included.

Hardware assisted virtualization is an example of platform virtualization. It uses assistance from the hardware to provide full virtualization, so unmodified guest operating systems can be supported. The technique was first used on IBM System/370 mainframe machines in 1972.

Virtualization is done with a second stage of address translation with its own page tables. I/O can be virtualized. The Hypervisor runs in a new privilege mode, unique to it. The mode is entered with a Hypervisor Call, instead of the previous Hypervisor Trap. The Virtualization privilege mode is a new third privilege level. There is the user code level, the operating system level, the Hypervisor level, and a TrustZone Privilege level, at the top. The Embedded Xen product supports virtualization on the ARM architecture.

In the ARM scheme, before virtualization, the Operating System controls the memory resource. Now, there is a second level of address translation. Where virtual addresses used to map to physical addresses, they now map to Intermediate addresses, which are then mapped to physical addresses by the Hypervisor.

Interrupts are another issue. An interrupt might need to go to the current or another guest operating system, the Hypervisor, or an operating system in the TrustZone. Physical interrupts go to the Hypervisor first; if they need to go to a guest operating system, this is handled by a "virtual" interrupt.

Since the ARM architecture uses memory-mapped I/O, that process is also virtualized. Virtual devices are created by emulation.

Cortex-R

The ARM Cortex-R has specific features to address performance in real-time applications. These include an instruction cache and a data cache, a floating point coprocessor, and an extended 8-stage pipeline. Cortex-R supports the Thumb and Thumb-2 instructions as well as ARM. Up to 64-bit data structures are supported. The compiler must be aware of which architecture is used as the code target, to introduce the proper optimizations for the various models. As with different implementations of the ISA-32 instruction set from Intel, different implementation architectures require different optimization strategies. The correct optimization for one chip could be the worst-case approach for a different implementation.

Cortex-M

Cortex M addresses microcontrollers. There are currently four models, the Cortex-M0, 1, 2, and 3. All are binary compatible. The M0 and M1 are based on the ARMv6, the M3 is based on the ARMv7, and the M4 is based on the ARM-V7-ME. The Thumb and Thumb-2 subsets are supported. The M3 model has a single cycle 32x32 hardware multiply and 10-12 cycle hardware divide instruction. The M4 adds Digital Signal Processing instructions such as a single-cycle 16/32 bit multiply-accumulate, and supports full Thumb and Thumb-2 instruction set. The IEEE-754 floating point unit is included with the M4. A nested, vectored interrupt controller is included. The 256 interrupts are fully deterministic, and an NMI is included. Cortex-M does not support the instruction and data caches, or the coprocessor interface, and has only a 3-stage pipeline. Only the M3 and M4 models support the Memory Protection Unit. The M3 instruction set provides a pair of synchronization primitives for a guaranteed atomic read-modify-write operation, which is critical to real-time operating systems.

Examples of the chip include the Atmel SAM3 series and the TI Stellaris models. These include flash and sram, timers including a real-time clock and watchdog, PWM for motor control, Ethernet, CAN, USB, and UART functions, and A/D's. The M4 models are made by Atmel, Freescale, STMicroelectronics, and TI.

The SPEAr1310 is an example of an implementation of the A9 architecture. There are numerous members of the SPEAr chip family, with single or multiple cores. The chips support SRAM and DRAM, NAND or NOR flash, Ethernet and giga-bit Ethernet, USB3, I^2C, I^2S, SPI, UART, HDLC, RS-485, CAN, IrDA, and PCIe/SATA, depending on the specific model.

The SPEAr300 models operate with a single core, up to 400 MHz, have 8-channel DMA, and include a real-time clock. Various I/O configurations are supported. The SPEAr600 models also operate to 400 MHz, but with dual cores. The 1310 model includes a (double data rate) DDR-3 memory interface. DDR-x memory is a variation of SDRAM. DDR-3 uses a 64 bit transfer, and supports up to 8 gigabytes. The 1340 model adds a GPU with 2D and 3D acceleration, and a hardware video encoder/decoder.

ARM 64

ARM architecture version 8 (ARMv8) defines support for 64-bit data and addressing, and multicore operations. It is dual-issue superscalar, so almost twice as many instructions per clock can be executed. All instructions are 32-bits, allowing for more rapid decode. There are 31 general purpose registers. It can include the NEON SIMD instruction set extension, and a vector floating point unit. It supports the Jazelle architecture. Branches are optimized with an advanced branch predictor that can achieve success rates approaching 95%. The virtual address space is 48 bits, with a 40-bit physical address space supported initially. The ARM v8 ISA allows for operation in 32-bit and 64-bit modes. It includes virtualization support, NEON SIMD support, and enhanced security, while maintaining compatibility with ARMv7.

The Version 8 has found application in the Apple A4, and is implemented at this writing by Freescale Semiconductor, Samsung, TI, and others. This architecture will supplement the ARM architectures dominance in smart phones, tablets, and embedded systems, with competition in top-end desktop and server applications.

ARM embedded

Embedded computing refers to special purpose computers that are a part of a larger system, as opposed to generic desktop computers, tablets, and servers. Embedded systems are for specific purposes; they are not necessarily general purpose. They may have a limited or no human interface, but usually support complex I/O. They form the basis of all modern technical devices.

The embedded computer can be characterized by the parameters of its central processing unit (CPU), memory, and input/output (I/O). The CPU parameters of importance are speed, power consumption, word size, and price. The memory parameters include power consumption, volatility, and size or capacity. I/O characteristics must be matched to those of external systems components.

The trend now is to include more than one CPU on the chip, called Multicore technology. In addition, specialized processor units for floating point, vector processing, and digital signal processing are included. Multicore changes the game.

Many embedded systems are required to be real-time - they have strict deadlines. Others are event-driven - a trigger event kicks off a predetermined sequence of responses. Embedded systems are almost always resource constrained. The resources might be size, weight, power, throughput, heat generation, reliability, deadlines, etc. Embedded systems have a high non-recurring engineering (NRE) cost (development cost), but are generally cheap to produce in volume.

Microcontrollers, where the CPU is combined with memory and I/O, represent most of the current implementations of the ARM. There are many different instantiations of the ARM in embedded applications. The embedded applications usually take advantage of a real-time operating system. System resources are an issues, particularly size, weight, and power. Applications include automotive, entertainment systems, medical devices, and industrial control. Fail-safe systems are part of the embedded world. Most of the processors manufacturing and sold are embedded, as opposed to desktop or server, by a wide margin. This section will discuss several selected examples of ARMs targeted to embedded applications. The features of the core, and the specific I/O interfaces, are tailored to fit the targeted application space. There are a very large number of devices available in this area. The ones discussed are typical.

Peripherals and memory reside on the same chip as the cpu or cpu's. Memory is genrraly SRAM for data, and flash, for programs. We need to discuss some of the common peripherals included on microcontrolers.

Embedded microcontrollers have one or more cpus, memory, and I/O on one chip. The different mixes depend on the manufacturer, and intended use of the chip. With a lot more transistors to use, modern embedded microcontrollers have a wide variety of I/O.

The functions onboard the chip may include a memory management unit, a multichannel dma controller, a priority interrupt controller, and may channels of general purpose I/O (GPIO). This can usually be configured on a bit basis to be input only, output only, or bi-directional. It can be used a multiple serial channels, or as a parallel port.

Special purpose serial I/O can also be provided, adding protocols on top of the serial bit stream. This is used for interfaces such as Ethernet, USB, RS-232/-422/–423, Firewire, Spacewire, MIL-STD-1553, or Controller Area Network (CAN). A hardware Universal Asynchronous Receiver Transmitter (UART) can also be easily implemented in either hardware or software. At the board level, the various required voltage and current levels are handled by receivers and drivers.

Joint Test Action Group (JTAG) is the name for the IEEE-1149.1 standard for a test access point and a boundary scan architecture for integrated circuit level debug. The JTAG effort began in 1985 as a test and fault isolation methodology for board level products. It is particularly valuable for embedded systems, with limited human interfaces for visibility. It is used in cpu-based systems, FPGA's, and SoC architectures. With the proper application software, the JTAG can access and control test instrumentation included within the chip. JTAG can also be used to load data into internal flash memory. JTAG is used a portal to the chips built-in self test (BIST).

JTAG uses a 4-wire interface (data in, data out, clock, mode select), sometimes with a 5th line, test reset. The data transfer mode is serial, using a short cable. The host side for the JTAG system can be connected via USB or even Ethernet. There are numerous commercial JTAG tool vendors providing multi-platform support, and Open Source tools also exist. Almost all modern embedded architectures provide JTAG support. A 2-wire alternative is Serial Wire Debug, that has the JTAG protocol implemented.

The *Serial Peripheral Interface* (SPI) bus is a full-duplex synchronous serial communication system. It is a master/slave architecture. It uses four wires for the serial clock, the Master-in/slave-out, the master-out/slave-in, and a slave-select. It is the basis for the *JTAG* (Joint Test Action Group)'s diagnostic interface, and has found application in general I/O device interfacing as well. Microwire is a SPI predecessor, that is half-duplex.

The *Inter-Integrated Circuit* (I^2C) bus is designed for short-range communication between chips on a board. It is a 2-wire interface that is multi-master, and bidirectional. There are 7-bit slave addresses, so 128 unique devices can be addressed from the current master. It was developed by Philips Semiconductor in the 1980's. It is widely used in embedded systems.

Another included feature may be analog input and output. This means the microcontroller has some analog circuitry onboard. This includes multichannel analog to digital (A/D) and digital to analog (D/A) ports.

The general purpose I/O pins can also sometimes be configured to generate an interrupt automatically when data becomes available, or the state of a pin changes.

From the GPIO capability, more comples functions can be implemented (in hardware) such as pulse-width modulation for device control. Software can reconfigure GPIO functions on the fly.

A counter/timer is invaluable in embedded systems. In timer mode, the input clock is the system or cpu clock. The counter is preloaded with a value, and counts down. When the count reaches zero, an interrupt is generated, and the counter register is reloaded. For example, with an 8-bit counter, if it is pre-loaded with 128, it generates a square wave at a system clock/256 rate. This allows periodic interrupts at sub-multiples of the system clock, and synchronous with it. We can also increment a second counter upon each interrupt to handle longer periods of elapsed time.

In counter mode, the clock comes from an external source, and is asynchronous to the system clock. For example, we might use the output stream of pulses from an optical encoder. Another application might be as the Baud rate clock for a serial I/O line.

Since the counter/timer usually has multiple channels, we might use one channel to generate a known time base, and other units for counting.

A special-purpose timer essential for embedded applications is the Watchdog. This is a free-running timer that generates a cpu reset unless it is reset by the software. This helps to ensure that the system doesn't lock up during certain critical time periods, and the software is meeting its deadlines. This approach has saved many a system.

If the watchdog is not reset, it generates an interrupt to reset the host. This should take the system back to a baseline state, and restart it. Hopefully, normal operations will resume. The embedded system can't rely on a human operator to notice a fault in the operations or a "hung" system, and press the reset button. The watchdog timer is implemented in hardware, and does it's jobs without direct software intervention. If the software fails to reset the timer, the system reboots. This might simply reset operations and restart, or may include diagnostics before the system is restarted.

For real-time systems, we need a good clock. This is used by the priority scheduler in the operating system to get the right software running at the right time.

Selected ARM architectures

This section discusses a small subset of the available ARM processors.

STMicroelectronics manufactures the STM32F line of 32-bit ARM Cortex models for embedded applications. These are embedded computers, including CPU, memory, and I/O. There are more than 100 variants with different performance and peripherals to address a broad spectrum of applications.

The STM 32F103 is a typical 32-bit MCU in the ARM Cortex line. It has the M3 core, and runs at a maximum frequency of 72 MHz. It includes 20 kbytes of SRAM, and up to 128 kbytes of flash memory. The SRAM operates at the CPU clock speed. It has power-on reset, which loads the program counter with the value in the reset vector which is at memory address 4.. A 32 KHz oscillator is included for the real-time clock. The clock maintains time and date, and can provide an alarm interrupt or periodic interrupt. Three low power modes are implemented: sleep, stop, and standby. In sleep mode, the cup clock is stopped but the peripherals are awake, and can awaken the CPU. Stop mode has all of clocks stopped. Content of the SRAM and registers are maintained. The chip can be awakened with the EXTI line, a non-maskable external interrupt. Standby mode has the lowest power consumption. Memory and register contents are lost. Standby mode is exited with a WKUP external signal or a NRST. The real time clock can also force an exit from Standby; its clock is not stopped in that mode.

The chip includes dual 12-bit analog to digital converters, with up to 16 channels available by multiplexing. There are seven channels of DMA available with timers, USARTS, and SPI and I2C support on I/O channels. There are a maximum of 80 map-able I/O ports that can be configured, and 16 vectored external interrupts. At reset, the vector table is at address 0. The chip runs on 3.3 volts, but the inputs are mostly 5 volt tolerant. A JTAG debugging port is available. There are three 16-bit timers that can be used for quadrature encoder input, or PWM output, and two watchdog timers. The 16-bit general purpose timers can count up or down, and have a capture/compare feature. The watchdog timer is independent of the main clock.

Standard communication interfaces that are supported include I²C, USART, SPI at 18 mbps), CAN, and USB 2.0. One or two I2C buses can be supported in multi-master or slave modes. The USART interface operates up to 4.5 Mbps, and can use DMA. The SPI interface can operate to 18 Mbps in full duplex and master mode. Can bus supports 2.0A and B formats to 1 Mbps, and uses frames with 11- or 29-bit identifiers. The USB interface goes to 12 Mbps. The chip includes a CRC calculation circuit with a 96-bit capacity. The STM32F represents a family chips, with low-, medium-, and high density models. Higher density models include more memory and I/O devices. The STM 32F103 is considered a medium density device. The chip can be configured to boot from system memory, user flash, or internal SRAM.

Any of the general purpose I/O pins can be software configured to be an input or an output. The ARM architecture uses memory-mapped I/O. The two built-in analog-digital converters share 16 channels, and include sample and hold. The chip also has an internal temperature sensor with a voltage that varies linearly with temperature. This is connected internally to ADC channel 12, input 16.

Maple

The Maple from LeafLabs is an Arduino-derived ARM architecture using the STM32F103RBT6, a 32-bit ARM Cortex M3 microprocessor. It is implemented on a 2 x 2 inch board, the design of which is open source It operates at 72 MHz, and has 128 KB of flash and 20 KB of SRAM. There are 43 digital I/O pins (GPIOs), 15 PWM pins at 16 bit resolution, and 15 analog input (ADC) pins at 12-bit resolution. It includes 2 SPI peripherals; 2 I²C peripherals, 7 Channels of DMA, and three USART (serial port) peripherals. There is one advanced and three general-purpose timers, and a dedicated USB port for programming and communications, which also supplies power. JTAG support is included. There is a Nested Vectored Interrupt Controller (NVIC).

LM3S9B92

The LM3S9B92 microcontroller chip from Texas Instruments uses the ARM Cortex-3 core plus the Thumb-2 instruction set. It is a member of TI's Stellaris product family. It implements single-cycle hardware multiply and divide, and supports unaligned data access. It has separate buses for instructions and data. Interrupt handling is deterministic, always being 12 cycles. Memory protection is provided. The chip is optimized for single-cycle flash memory. It supports a 80-MHz clock. It has a 24-bit integrated system timer, a vectored interrupt controller with an NMI and dynamically re-prioritizable interrupts.

The microcontroller includes 96 kbytes of single cycle RAM on chip and 256 kbytes of single cycle flash. Flash blocks of 1-kbyte in size can be marked as read-only or execute-only. The I/O can support 10/100 Ethernet, 2 CAN controllers, USB 2.0, three UART's, dual I^{2}C, and dual synchronous serial. There are four 32-bit timers, eight PWM's, two watchdog timers, and up to 65 general purpose I/O's. Two quadrature encoder inputs are provided for motor feedback. There are two 10-bit A/D's with 16 shared channels. In additional, there are three analog comparators that can generate an interrupt. JTAG is supported.

Raspberry Pi

The Raspberry Pi is a small, inexpensive, single board computer based on the ARM architecture. It is targeted to the academic market. It uses the Broadcom BCM2835 system-on-a-chip, which has a 700 MHz ARM processor, a video GPU, and currently 512 M of RAM. It uses an SD card for storage. The Raspberry Pi runs the GNU/linux and FreeBSD operating systems. It was first sold in February 2012. Sales reached ½ million units by the Fall. Due to the open source nature of the software, Raspberry Pi applications and drivers can be downloaded from various sites. It requires a single power supply, and dissipates less than 5 watts. It has USB ports, and an Ethernet controller. It does not have a real-time clock, but one can easily be added. It outputs video in HDMI resolution, and supports audio output. I/O includes 8 general purpose I/O lines, UART, I2C bus, and SPI bus.

The Raspberry Pi design belongs to the Raspberry Pi Foundation in the UK, which was formed to promote the study of Computer Science. The Raspberry Pi is seen as the successor to the original BBC Microcomputer by Acorn, which resulted in the ARM processor. The unit has enough resources to host an operating system such as linux.

The latest model is the Pi 2 Model B at this writing. It uses an ARM v7 quadcore processor (the Broadcom BCM2836) and has a gigabyte of ram. The chip includes a graphics processing unit (GPU), the VideoCore IV, that operates independently of the CPU's. This is supported by an open source library of image processing routines.

The board supports the usb interface, ethernet, HDMI video, and a digital camera direct interface. A microSDHC card is used for program storage. It runs a variation of Debian Linux.

The Raspberry Pi Zero is a $5 board that offers a 1 GHz cpu, 512 megabytes of ram, and uses a usb interface and a micro-SD card slot. It includes HDMI video. It runs Linux.

Application domains

Ford Sync Telematics System

The Ford Sync is a vehicle infotainment systems based on an ARM processor. It is a factory installed feature, first available on 2008 model year vehicles. The system allows the driver to use Bluetooth-enabled devices such as phones and media players in the vehicle, and operate these with voice command or steering wheel based controls. The steering wheel has, for example, a push-to-talk button for connected phones. The SYNC system also provides a text-to-voice feature for reading messages aloud.

Integration of digital music players can be via Bluetooth or USB connection. A voice recognition feature is implemented in the SYNC system, and it supports English, French, Spanish, and Brazilian Portuguese. Direct calling to 911 in case of emergency is supported.

The operating system is Microsoft's Windows Embedded Automotive. The SYNC uses proprietary software. Certain BlackBerry, Android, or iPhone apps can be triggered by the steering wheel buttons, or voice command.

The computer hosting SYNC is the Accessory Protocol Interface Module (APIM), which interfaces with vehicle systems over the CAN bus. The initial implementation of SYNC used a 400 MHz Freescale ARM-11 processor, with 256 Mbytes of SDRAM, and 2 Gbytes of flash.

iPad2, iPhone4S, iPod Touch 5th gen

Apple has used the ARM architecture in their mobiles products for some time, as in the A5 system-on-a-chip, designed by Apple, and fabricated by Samsung. This is a Cortex A9 architecture, running up to 1 GHz, with dynamic clocking, for power reduction. It includes the L1 and L2 cache, 512 megabytes of DRAM, and is a dual core unit. Specialized units for face detection for the camera, and noise cancellation for the microphone are included.

Arduino

The Arduino is open source microcomputer hardware. There are a multitude of variations, using different underlying software. The Arduino Due was the first to use the ARM architecture, a Cortex-M3 core. It is a 4 x 2.1 inch board with 512 kilobytes of flash, 96 kilobytes of SRAM54 digital I/O pins, and 12 analog inputs. It was released in 2012, and operates at 84 MHz.

ARM IP

ARM Holdings, Ltd. is the IP (Intellectual Property) holder for the ARM architecture. ARM Cores are not hardware; they are packages of Intellectual Property, essentially design data for an system that can be instantiated in a devices such as a field programmable gate array (FPGA). Multiple pieces of IP from different sources can be combined in one device to implement a customized system-on-a-chip. Different IP Cores, as building blocks, are licensed and controlled differently. The IP is the copyright and patent covering the design elements. Once developed, an IP core can be provided as a standard system element for multiple purposes. Open source IP cores are also available (http://opencores.org/), including ARM-compatible units. Open source cores are frequently provided under the GPL (gnu public license).

Applications of ARM cores include the Game Boy Advance, Nintendo DS, Apple iPod, Lego NXT, various Garmin Navigation Devices, the Hewlett-Packard HP-49/50 Calculators, TomTom navigation devices, Canon EOS 5D digital camera, Zaurus SL-5600, Gumstix basix, Palm Tungsten, Blackberry 8700, Blackberry Pearl (8100), Apple iPhone (original and 3G), Apple iPod touch (1st and 2nd Generation), Nintendo 3DS, Nokia N900, and others.

Applications of licensed ARM cores in System-on-chip (SOC) designs provide a quick time to market for commercial products in volume markets. SOC's will include the CPU, memory, and specialized I/O in one package. Analog circuitry can also be included.

Cores are similar to software libraries. This characterizes the soft core, a hardware description language (HDL) description of the core. Hardware description languages such as Verilog or VHDL are used. The user can modify the design (within the rights granted by the core owner.) It is, essentially, source code for the hardware. The core can also be supplied as a netlist, a set of logical functions implemented in generic gates. A gate-level netlist is often compared to assembly language for hardwarer.

Hard cores are physical descriptions of the device, essentially, transistor-level descriptions. These have the advantage of having timing and performance determinism. Usually, the hard cores are targeted to a specific foundry.

Various complications are encountered in licensing IP cores to government organizations as opposed to companies, because of restrictions on electronics for defense or weapons systems.

Counterfeiting of parts, and backdoors in the hardware are also current areas of security concern.

ARM Multicore

The latest ARM architecture supports multicore (currently, up to 8-core) architectures. Both symmetrical and asymmetrical implementations are included. Putting a lot of cores on a single substrate is challenging, but getting them to work together co-operatively and non-intrusively is difficult. The CoreLink cache coherent interconnect system IP, for use in multicore applications, is one emerging solution. Some problems are inherently parallelizable, but most are not. Not many problem domains scale linearly with the amount of computing horsepower available. Embarrassingly parallel applications are rarely of practical interest.

The Cortex-A9 microarchitecture comes with either a scalable multicore processor, the Cortex-A9 MPCore™ multicore processor, or as a more traditional processor, the Cortex-A9 single core processor. The configuration includes 16, 32, or 64KB four-way associative L1 caches, with up to 8MB of L2 cache through the optional L2 cache controller. The memory architecture of the A9 is Harvard, with separate code and data paths. It can sustain four double-word write transfers every 5 cycles. It includes a high efficiency superscalar pipeline, which removes dependencies between adjacent instructions. It has double the floating point performance of previous units. Up to a 2 GHz clock is currently feasible. Two instructions per cycle are decoded. Instruction execution is speculative, using dynamic register renaming. A similar technique is used to unroll loops in the hardware at execution time. There are four execution pipelines fed from the issue queue, and out-of-order dispatch is supported, as is out-of-order write-back. Items can be marked as non-cachable, or write back or write through.

Cache Coherency in Multicore

In multicore architectures, each CPU core may have its own L1 cache, but share L2 caches with other cores. Local data in the L1 caches must be consistent with data in other L1 caches. If one core changes a value in cache due to a write operation, that data needs to be changed in other caches as well (if they hold the same item).

This problem is well known and studies from the field of multiprocessing. The issues can be addressed by several mechanisms. In cache snooping, each cache monitors the others for changes. If a change in value is seen, the local cached copy is invalidated. This means it will have to be re-accessed from the next level before use. A global directory of cached data can also be maintained. Several protocols for cache coherency include MSI, MESI, others.

ARM SoC

A system-on-a-chip includes the processor, memory, and I/O on a single chip. These may be on different die, though. Analog and radio frequency parts can be included. The SoC is a "one-chip" solution. As semiconductor manufacturing technology advances, more functionality can be provided on a single chip. An alternative approach is the System in a Package (SiP), which integrates multiple die on one package,

Most SOC design starts with IP cores and hardware blocks that are pre-qualified and tested. These could include ARM Cores as IP. These can be combined in the design with memory cores, and specific I/O cores such as USB and CAN. Each core comes with its own license terms and restrictions. SOC's can be fabricated as full custom chips, in standard cells, and in FPGA's. The non-recurring engineering (NRE) costs are higher for the SOC approach, but it can result in a highly optimized design in terms of space, power, and reliability.

Standard cell libraries are available. These have the advantage of having been tested in silicon, and target certain foundries and processes. Typical components include the Cortex cores, multimedia, interconnect, and memory controller.

An example of an ARM-based SOC is the Apple A5, used in the iPad-2 and iPhone-4S. This is an ARM V7 architecture, with the chip fabricated by Samsung. It can use a single or dual CPU core, and has dual L1 and L2 cache. It includes the NEON SIMD accelerator at 1 GHz, a custom image signal processor for face recognition and 512 Mbytes of memory

Field Programmable Gate Arrays are integrated circuits that are programmable or configurable at the hardware level. The devices are ideal for high density embedded designs. This configuration defines the interconnect between standard logic blocks on the device. The logic blocks can also be configurable. The device can be set up to be programmed once, or capable of being programmed multiple times. In the limit, the device can be reconfigured on the fly, as it is operating. An FPGA gives us configurable instead of fixed hardware. A traditional CPU provides fixed hardware from the manufacturer that we can direct with a software program in terms of operations on data, and the sequence of these operations. It supports data-dependent branches. With an FPGA, we have "programmable" or configurable hardware as well. Each reconfiguration results in a new and different architecture.

IP Cores are design files allowing for instantiation of standard components in an ASIC or FPGA. A large market has developed in the marketing and licensing of IP Cores. The advantage of the IP Core from a reputable source is the standardized design file that has been verified. Cores for I/O functions and complete processors are available. Cores can contain both analog and digital functions. Open source IP cores are available. These allow for modification of the design. The ARM processor, among others, is available as an IP core.

IP Cores

An *intellectual property (IP)* core is a reusable logic unit that can be licensed, owned, and included in a design. IP cores can be used as building blocks for ASIC's, FPGA's, and Soc's. The discussion in the software section regarding proprietary versus open source applies. IP cores can also be proprietary or open source. Cores as a product are available in hardware description language form, essentially, source code for hardware. Proprietary cores may or may not be modifiable, and may or may not be supported by the vendor. Cores may also be available as netlist files, which are a Boolean algebra representation that has to be instantiated in a specific technology. A gate level netlist is seen as analogous to assembly language, and is portable to any process (implementation) technology.

The cores can contain digital and analog components, but the analog components require specific transistor layout formats. Complete embedded processors such as the 8-bit Intel 8051 series and various members of the ARM family are available as cores. Besides entire cpu's, IP cores are available for various interfaces and I/O devices. Individual developers can produce cores, and include them in libraries.

The intellectual property owner, the developer of the core, sees a return on his NRE cost of developing the hardware, and can have the design used in a large number of application areas, perhaps leading to an industry standard or industry-preferred approach. Core vendors are wary of reverse engineering of their core, just as software suppliers are concerned with the same process in their domain. Open Source cores are available.

Hard cores are defined at a physical layer, and provide a predictable performance. They are supplied as transistor-level layout format. This is subject to using a particular target chip foundry. Generally, a hard core cannot be changed. It represents a plug-in function. Soft cores, on the other hand, are specified in the RTL language, or as a netlist, and are "compiled" into a design. They can be easily changed by industry-standard toolsets. The design is portable, with respect to a fabrication technology.

CPU cores are readily available for popular CPU architectures. A PCIexpress bus core is available, as well as Ethernet, CAN bus, usb, and other standards. Various cores to address specific application areas such as DSP are also available.

Vector Floating Point

The ARM floating point functionality was implemented in software before ARM processors had built-in floating point hardware. The Vector floating point (VFP) hardware functionality support is enabled when the startup program detects the presence of the appropriate hardware and sets a system flag.

The VFP is disabled initially. Any access causes an undefined instruction exception, allowing the kernel to initialize the context for a thread. An exception is generated, and the kernel exception handler allocates storage for the context, initializes the state, marks the thread as owning the VFP, and restarts the instruction. VFP is disabled by a context switch to allow the kernel to trap subsequent accesses for managing the per-thread context. If the access is performed by the thread owning the VFP, it already contains the correct state. In this case, the VFP is simply re-enabled and the instruction is restarted. If the access is performed by a different thread, a context switch is required. The state is saved in the owning thread's storage. If this is the first access performed by the thread, storage is allocated for the context, and its state is initialized. The state is restored from the new thread's storage. The new thread is recorded as owning the VFP, and the instruction is restarted.

VFP support implements only the RunFast mode of operation, in which:

- trapped floating point exceptions are disabled
- the Round-to-nearest mode is enabled
- the Flush-to-zero mode is enabled
- default NaN's are enabled

Both Round-to-nearest and Flush-to-zero are defined in the IEEE-754 standard. This mode of operation doesn't require any software support code, but it doesn't provide full IEEE-754 compliance. Full details of the RunFast mode are given in the ARM Architecture Reference Manual.

No software emulation or support code is provided for the VFP instruction set. This means that code using VFP instructions can be run only on a processor that implements VFP hardware.

The standard QNX Neutrino libraries are compiled to use a soft-float implementation for floating-point operations to ensure the code can run on all supported ARM processors. The soft-float implementation passes floating-point arguments and results in ARM registers, or on the stack. The code that uses VFP instructions for floating point must use the same argument (or result mechanism) to ensure that it can interoperate correctly with code compiled for soft-float.

A VFP-enabled math library is provided and can be used on targets that implement VFP hardware. The startup program is responsible for detecting the presence of VFP hardware. ARM Floating Point architecture provides hardware support for floating point operations in half-, single- and double-precision floating point arithmetic. It is fully IEEE-754 compliant, with full software library support.

The floating point capabilities of the ARM VFP offer increased performance for floating point arithmetic used in automotive applications, imaging such as scaling, transforms and font generation in printing, 3D transforms, and FFT and filtering in graphics. Consumer products such as Internet appliances, set-top boxes, and home gateways, directly benefit from the ARM VFP.

Many real-time control applications in the industrial and automotive fields require the dynamic range and precision of floating-point. Automotive powertrain, anti-lock braking, traction control, and active suspension systems are all applications where precision and predictability are essential.

Hardware floating point is essential for many applications, and can be used as part of a System on Chip (SoC) design flow using high-level design tools (MatLab, MATRIXx and LabVIEW) to directly model the system and derive the application code. Combined with the NEON multimedia processing engine, hardware floating point can increase performance of high-end imaging applications such as scaling, 2D and 3D transforms, font generation, and digital filters.

There have been three main versions of VFP. VFPv1 is now obsolete. VFPv2 is an optional extension to the ARM instruction set in the ARMv5 and ARMv6 architectures. VFPv3 is an optional extension to the ARM, Thumb, and ThumbEE instruction sets in the ARMv7-A and ARMv7-R profiles. VFPv3 can be implemented with either 32 or 16 double word registers.

Media Processing

Media Processing refers to operations on audio and video data structures. These are Digital Signal Processing operations. Image compression and decompression operations on streaming video in real time is an example. NXP Semiconductors, N.V. of the Netherlands integrates ARM Cortex cores with their signal processing technology.

The ARM NEON is a general purpose SIMD engine operating on multimedia data structures. It has a 128-bit architecture, and serves as an extension for the ARM Cortex-A. It has sixteen 128-bit registers.

The Advanced SIMD extension, marketed as NEON technology, is a combined 64- and 128-bit single-instruction, multiple-data (SIMD) instruction set that provides standardized acceleration for media and signal processing applications. NEON can execute MP3 audio decoding on CPUs running at 10 MHz and can run the GSM AMR (Adaptive Multi-Rate) speech codec at no more than 13 MHz. It features a comprehensive instruction set, separate register files and independent execution hardware. NEON supports 8-, 16-, 32- and 64-bit integer and single-precision (32-bit) floating-point data and operates in SIMD operations for handling audio and video processing as well as graphics and gaming processing. In NEON, the SIMD supports up to 16 operations at the same time. The NEON hardware shares the same floating-point registers as used in VFP.

Open Source versus Proprietary

This is a topic we need to discuss before we get into software. It is not a technical topic, but concerns your right to use (and/or own) software. It's those software licenses you click to agree with, and never read. That's what the intellectual property lawyers are betting on.

Software and software tools are available in proprietary and open source versions. *Open source software* is free and widely available, and may be incorporated into your system. It is available under license, which generally says that you can use it, but derivative products must be made available under the same license. This presents a problem if it is mixed with purchased, licensed commercial software, or a level of exclusivity is required. Major government agencies such as the Department of Defense and NASA have policies related to the use of Open Source software.

Adapting a commercial or open source operating system to a particular problem domain can be tricky. Usually, the commercial operating systems need to be used "as-is" and the source code is not available. The software can usually be configured between well-defined limits, but there will be no visibility of the internal workings. For the open source situation, there will be a multitude of source code modules and libraries that can be configured and customized, but the process is complex. The user can also write new modules in this case.

Large corporations or government agencies sometimes have problems incorporating open source products into their projects. Open Source did not fit the model of how they have done business traditionally. They are issues and lingering doubts. NASA has created an open source license, the NASA Open source Agreement (NOSA), to address these issues. It has released software under this license, but the Free Software Foundation has some issues with the terms of the license. The Open Source Initiative (www.opensource.org) maintains the definition of Open Source, and certifies licenses such as the NOSA.

The GNU General Public License (GPL) is the most widely used free software license. It guarantees end users the freedoms to use, study, share, copy, and modify the software. Software that ensures that these rights are retained is called free software. The license was originally written by Richard Stallman of the Free Software Foundation (FSF) for the GNU project in 1989. The GPL is a copyleft license, which means that derived works can only be distributed under the same license terms. This is in distinction to permissive free software licenses, of which the BSD licenses are the standard examples. Copyleft is in counterpoint to traditional copyright. Proprietary software "poisons" the free software, and cannot be included or integrated with it, without abandoned the GPL. The GPL cover the GNU/linux operating systems and most of the GNU/linux-based applications.

A Vendor's software tools and Operating system or application code is usually proprietary intellectual property. It is unusual to get the source code to examine, at least without binding legal documents and additional funds. Along with this, you get the vendor support. An alternative is open source code, which is in the public domain. There are a series of licenses covering open source code usage, including the Creative Commons License, the gnu public license, copyleft (alternative to copyright), and others. Open Source describes a collaborative environment for development and testing. Use of open source code carries with it an implied responsibility to "pay back" to the community. Open Source is not necessarily free.

The Open source philosophy is sometimes at odds with the rigid-ized procedures evolved to ensure software performance and reliability. Offsetting this is the increased visibility into the internals of the software packages, and control over the entire software package. Besides application code, operating systems such as GNU/linux and bsd can be open source. The programming language Python is open source. The popular web server Apache is also open source.

ARM Software

Various operating systems are available for the ARM architecture, including variations of Gnu/GNU/linux and bsd. The Android operating is the basis for many ARM-based smart phones and tablets. Microsoft's Windows-RT (Version 8), released in 2012, targets the ARM architecture. In the embedded world, most real-time operating systems include ARM support. ARM's advantage in the software area is the presentation of a standard platform, which allows software reuse, and the development of libraries.

In the area of applications software and development, there is a natural synergy between Java and the ARM architecture. This is not to say that other languages such as c/c++ can't be used. A c language to byte code compiler exists, as does those for other languages. An ARM implementation does not need to support the ARM ISA, strangely enough. Data access is little- or big endian, with little-endian the default. The processor view of memory is that it is a linear structure of bytes, numbered in ascending order from zero. Supported data types include 8, 16, and 32-bit words. A programmer's view of the registers shows R0-R12 as general purpose, R13 as the stack pointer, R14 as the link register, and R15 as the program counter. R8 to R12 are not accessible by 16-bit instructions.

Java is an object-oriented language with a syntax similar to that of c. The language is compiled to bytecodes which are executed by a Java Virtual Machine (JVM). The JVM is hosted on the computer hardware, and is an instruction interpreter program. Thus, the Java language is independent of the hardware it executes on. The JVM has also been instantiated directly in hardware.

The JVM is a software environment that allows bytecodes to be executed. There are standard libraries to implement the applications programming interface (API). These implement the Java runtime environment. Other languages besides Java can be compiled into bytecode, notably Pascal, ADA, and Python. JVM is written in the c language.

The JVM can emulate and interpret the instruction set, or use a technique called Just in Time (JIT) compilation. The latter approach provides greater speed. The JVM also validates the bytecodes before execution.

The bytecode is interpreted or compiled. Java includes an API to make up the Java runtime environment. Oracle Corporation owns Java, but allows use of the trademark, as long as the products adhere to the JVM Specification. The JVM implements a stack-based architecture. Code executes as privileged or unprivileged, which limits access to some resources.

Numerous software tools and environments for the ARM exist, both proprietary and open source. These include tools from industry leaders such as Wind River (VxWorks), Green Hills, Mentor Graphics, QNX, and others. These are both development and debugging toolsets. Keil provides a software development environment for ARM, and ARM itself has a "development studio" for the chips.

ARM operating systems

The *Android* operating system by Google has found wide application in numerous ARM-based smartphone and tablet computers since its introduction in 2008. It is an Open Source product based on Gnu-GNU/linux, although not all of the code is covered by Open source licenses. It is evolving into versions for set-top boxes, phones, and digital television applications. Android supports multiple hardware computing platforms including ARM.

Like Java, Android provides a virtual machine execution engine for a given hardware platform. This virtual machine is termed Dalvik. Its strengths are in memory-limited systems, and those with hard real time requirements. Android is targeted to user input from touch, with a screen using icons. Android uses the Gnu-GNU/linux kernel, plus middleware, libraries of code, and API's. A large library of applications for Android is supported by the user community. Android has standard support for power management.

Dalvik is the process virtual machine for Google Android. It is being ported to other platforms as well. Applications in Java are compiled to byte code, but then are converted to Dalvik Executables. These are typically optimized for systems with limited speed and memory, such as cell phones. The Java Virtual Machine is a stack architecture with 8-bit instructions, but the Dalvik Virtual machine is a traditional register architecture, with 16-bit instructions. Dalvik also supports a just-in-time compiler. Dalvik is an open-source product.

FreeRTOS, and open source product, runs on the Raspberry Pi.

The ARM architecture is also supported by the various versions of the bsd operating systems, and Ubuntu and Debian GNU/GNU/linux, among others. The popular Raspberry Pi ARM-based board runs FreeBSD and Debian Gnu/GNU/linux. A version of Microsoft's Windows-8 is targeted to the ARM, and is called Windows-RT. It is the basis of Microsoft's *Surface* tablet. Real time operating systems for the ARM include Lynx-OS, QNX Neutrino, Keil's RTX, VxWorks, and many others.

IOS is the proprietary mobile operating system developed by Apple for their ARM-based phones and tablets. It was first released in 2007. It is not available outside Apple, or on non-Apple hardware. There is a Software Development Kit available for developers from Apple. IOS is derived from OS-X, which is in turn derived from the Darwin software. It is not to be confused with the software of the same name from Cisco, used in its routers.

Microsoft released a version of their proprietary embedded Windows software for the ARM-based consumer electronics, specifically the Windows Phone. This was a derivative of Windows-CE (compact edition).

NASA has embraced the concept of Open Source, even for certain mission critical applications. The Core Flight Executive, the key component of onboard computer software, was developed in the C language, and is open source. It has been show to run on the Raspberry Pi, although it is usually hosted on a custom, radiation-hardened machine.

In a real-time system, the timing of the result is as important as the logical correctness. Embedded systems find themselves in these situations a lot. There are two types of deadlines, hard and soft, and various scheduling policies to address these. A scheduling policy should have the ability to meet all deadlines. The scheduling overhead should be minimal.

In soft real time, the average performance or response time is emphasized. Desktops and servers can meet soft real time requirements. Missing a deadline is not necessarily catastrophic. It may result in a degradation of service, but not a failure.

In hard real time, on the other hand, critical sections of code have absolute deadlines, regardless of how busy the system is. Missing a deadline means system failure. Response times must be deterministic. Examples of hard real time systems include most spacecraft avionics.

Interestingly, meeting a deadline early may be just as bad as meeting it late. There may be constraint requirements on the response time window for the systems, and too many resources consumed in being early that make other processes late.

We can have systems with the characteristics of both; these multi-rate systems handle operations and deadlines at varying rates.

Non-Real Time (NRT) systems are fair; they provide resources (time, I/O) to all users or programs on an equal, or pre-determined priority basis. They can arbitrate resource allocation to maximize the number of deadlines met, or minimize lateness, or some combination. Everyone gets a turn. NRT systems have high throughput and fast average response.

Multiple approaches to scheduling have evolved, and we'll discuss some of them here.

In Round Robin scheduling, we can bound maximum CPU load, but may leave unused CPU cycles. The scheduling can be adapted to handle an unexpected load. We want to use all the available time slots by the end of period. We will schedule tasks that are ready, and use equal time intervals. Of course, if a ready low priority task can lock out a not-yet-ready high priority task, we have a problem. This is not a good approach for hard real time.

Not all CPU time is available for processes, some is used for operating system overhead. The scheduling process itself consumes CPU time. Scheduling overhead must be taken into account for the exact schedule.

To evaluate and define the worst case, we need to examine the requirements, and the implementation design in terms of the cpu, the program that is running, the specific task that is addressing the worst case, the context of the operating system, and other software activities. We can ensure meeting deadlines by hardware or software, or both. We can develop faster or smarter software, or choose faster hardware.

One approach is the use of a cyclic executive. Here, a timer triggers a task every frame. This is a periodic interrupt. Timers are the on-chip peripherals that are used by the scheduler.

When using event driven programming, some events are asynchronous to the system, and the embedded system must react to them. We determine our latency requirements and program our system accordingly. However, many events need to be tightly synchronized to a specific clock.

Timers allow us to perform event-driven operations on an accurate time-scale without tying up our processor, providing deterministic performance. Timers give us greater time resolution than we could accomplish (easily at least) using sequential programming techniques.

We need to generate a predefined list of tasks that the systems will accomplish, based on the system requirements. If we need concurrency, we will require a synchronization mechanism. We are trying to achieve a predictive response under all conditions. We also need to know data dependencies between processes. We need to profile the software to define the execution times, average and worst case.

There are multiple *real time scheduling policies*, which are tailored to the application domain and its requirements. Each task has an associated priority.

The resources are allocated to the highest priority task that is ready. Priorities determine the scheduling process. Priorities can be fixed or time-varying. The problem becomes whether the system can meet all required deadlines. One solution is to increase the cpu speed. You do this by waiting for the next generation of hardware. But, faster systems can also consume more power, and dissipate more heat.

We also may have *aperiodic processes*, which execute on demand, controlled by asynchronous external processes.

In the *Fixed Priority Preemptive scheme*, a higher priority task can preempt a lower priority task. In the *Rate Monotonic* scheme, the higher the frequency of a task, the higher its priority.

We always need to keep in mind the context switch overhead; there is a finite amount of time and resources required to switch tasks (or threads of execution). This is the task switch overhead.

Real-time tasks share resources for which they contend, and they may be forced to wait.

Priority inheritance protocols bound priority inversion. Real time operating systems generally use a priority based preemptive scheduler. Each task has a unique priority based on system requirements. Tasks have an associated state, running, ready, or waiting. A scheduler program ensures that of the list of ready tasks, the highest priority one is running. A lower priority task may be preempted. A problem may occur because of shared resources. In *priority inversion*, the highest priority task fails to run when it should due to a shared resource conflict.

Priority inversion was demonstrated on the surface of Mars in July 1977 during the Pathfinder Mission. A higher priority task was forced to wait for a lower priority task, due to shared resource contention. A lower priority task had control of a resource that it needed to access until completion. This locked out the critical higher resource task. It was successfully identified and fixed, remotely.

In unbounded priority inversion, we have multiple medium priority tasks. The tasks are periodic. If we have a lower priority task holding a critical resource, and a medium priority tasks preempt the lower priority task, which can't complete, we have a problem. And, since the tasks are periodic, they keep getting rescheduled, and the problem continues.

In a priority inheritance protocol, a task runs at its original priority, unless it is blocking a higher priority task. Then, it runs at the priority of the higher level task it is blocking. Mutual deadlocks are possible; this is the deadly embrace scenario. Here, neither task can proceed until the other allows it.

In the *Priority ceiling* protocol, no task can be blocked for longer than the duration of the longest critical section of a lower priority task, instead of for the entire duration of the lower priority task. Aperiodic tasks are non-periodic events with no fixed deadlines, but they interfere with periodic tasks.

Soft Realtime

Operating Systems designed for the desktop are not necessarily suited to the embedded space. They were developed under the assumption that whatever resources are required will be available. They are also *fair* in the sense of allocating resources without priorities. These are fine for desktop applications and servers, even some soft real time systems. Both proprietary and Open Source operating systems are applicable for soft real time systems. Be careful in their use, because they bring a lot of functions along with them that are not applicable to the embedded world.

One open source solution is a clever Linux distribution called Linux from Scratch. This is a bottoms-up approach to generating a custom Linux distribution. For the desktop, you generally get a Linux with just about everything included, and add to it what you need. In the embedded world, you need a lean-and-mean operating system. With Linux from Scratch, you only include the modules you need. If your spacecraft has no video, you don't need to include video drivers in the package. There is a learning curve in building operating systems from modules, but it is an interesting approach to optimization.

Hard real time

Real-time operating systems, as opposed to those addressing desktop, tablet, and server applications, emphasize predictability and consistency over throughput and low latencies. Determinism is probably the most important feature in a real-time operating system.

A microkernel operating system is ideally suited to embedded systems. It is slimmed down to include only those features needed, with no additional code. Barebones is the term often used. The microkernel handles memory management, threads, and communication between processes. It has device drivers for only those devices present. The operating systems may have to be recompiled when new devices are added. A file system, if required, is run in user space. MINIX, as an example of a streamlined open-source kernel, and has about 6,000 lines of code.

The ARM supports a series of real time operating systems, among them...

Programmer's View

The ARM supports a 32-bit ISA and various extensions ISA's such as Thumb (16-bit), Thumb-II (32-bit) and others. Not all implementations necessarily include all of these.

The 16-bit ISA presents a basic load/store approach with math and logic operations. Bit operations and conditional or unconditional branches are included. The multiply operation uses values in registers. There is no divide operation. The 32-bit ISA has the same basic operations on 32-bit data, with some extended operations. A 32-bit entity is a word, a 64-bit entity is a double-word, 16-bits is a half-word, and 8 bits is a byte.

Data access is little- or big-endian, set by the state of a CPU pin at reset. Code access is little-endian.

The Thumb ISA is a subset of the ARM ISA, giving better code density for commonly used operations.

Operation modes include Thread and Handler. Handler mode is used for interrupts or exceptions, and is executed in privileged mode. An interrupt comes from an external source, and an exception comes from an internal source, such as an overflow. Thread mode has both privileged (system) and user submodes. The user mode supports application code.

The 32-bit register set includes the 13 general purpose registers R0-R12, the stack pointer R13, the link register R14, the program counter R15, and a Program Status Register (PSR). The program counter always has bit zero set equal to zero. R0 to R7 can be accessed by the 16-bit instructions, but R8-R12 are restricted to access by the 32-bit instructions.

The PSR has five user-readable flags, with 27 reserved bits. The flags are set and cleared automatically during instruction execution, and reflect state information. Bit 31 of the PSR is the Negative flag, bit 30 is the Zero flag, bit 29 is carry/borrow, bit 28 is overflow, and bit 27 is Q, the sticky saturation flag. This flag indicates that saturation has not occurred since the last reset.

Java byte codes are hardware-independent instructions. Actually, these are the opcodes of the Java Virtual Machine (JVM). The byte codes are of course 8-bit in size, but opcodes can be multi-byte. These were defined by Sun Microsystems, the inventor of Java. The language is now owned and licensed by Oracle. A Java compiler outputs byte codes from Java language source code. One can program directly in bytecodes; this is like assembly language.

The idea behind Java was to define a language for a virtual machine, not actual hardware. This language would be compiled to byte codes, and executed by emulation software, the JVM, implemented on any and all CPU hardware. Actually, the JVM was instantiated in real hardware to make a Java "chip." Java processors can execute the bytecodes directly; they do not need to be emulated in a JVM. (see the Jazelle approach).

Java is an object-oriented language, and has the standard arithmetic and logical operation primitives, plus flow-of-control instructions. There are specific opcodes for object-oriented operations, such as object create and manage. Of course, other languages can also be compiled to byte codes for execution by a JVM.

ARM in Space

There have been numerous space projects utilizing the ARM processor. Among these, the Surrey Satellite Technology Nanosat Applications Platform (SNAP-1), which was launched on June 28, 2000. The onboard computer (OBC) was based on Intel's StrongARM SA-1100 with 4 Mbytes of 32-bit wide EDAC protected SRAM. The error correction logic corrected 2 bits in every 8 using a modified Hamming code and the errors are flushed from memory by software to prevent accumulation from multiple single-event upsets. There was 2 Mbytes of Flash memory containing a simple bootloader. The bootloader loads the application software into SRAM.

To be used in a mission-critical application in space, the processor has to be insensitive to radiation damage. This involves both circuit-level and architectural (implementation) techniques for radiation hardening against both total dose and transient events, such as single event upsets (SEU's). These areas are fairly well understood, and techniques such as TMR (triple modular redundancy) and error detection and correction codes are employed. These techniques apply not only to the CPU, but also the memory and I/O circuitry as well.

Radiation hard circuitry can find application in terrestrial applications as well, for nuclear reaction control, research particle accelerators, and high-energy scanning devices, particularly for medical devices.

ARM architecture implemented in inherently radiation hard technologies is an ongoing research area.

The ARM processor has found usage in the new area of Cubesats. A Cubesat is a small, affordable satellite that can be developed and launched by college, high schools, and even individuals. The specifications were developed by Academia in 1999. The basic structure is a 10 centimeter cube, (volume of 1 liter) weighing less that 1.33 kilograms. This allows a series of these standardized packages to be launched as secondary payloads on other missions. A Cubesat dispenser has been developed, the Poly-PicoSat Orbital Deployer, that holds multiple Cubesats and dispenses them on orbit. They can also be launched from the Space Station, via a custom airlock. ESA, the United States, and Russia provide launch services. The Cubesat origin lies with Prof. Twiggs of Stanford University and was proposed as a vehicle to support hands-on university-level space education and opportunities for low-cost space access.

Cubesats can be custom made, but there has been a major industry evolved to supply components, including space computers. It allows for an off-the-shelf implementation, in addition to the custom build. There is quite a bit of synergy between the Amsat folks and Cubesats. NASA supports the Cubesat program, holding design contests providing a free launch to worthy projects. Cubesats are being developed around the world, and several hundred have been launched.

A simple Cubesat controller can be developed from a standard embedded platform such as the Arduino. The lack of radiation hardness can be balanced by the short on-orbit lifetime. The main drivers for a Cubesat flight computer are small size, small power consumption, wide functionality, and flexibility. In addition, a wide temperature range is desirable. The architecture should support a real time operating system, but, in the simplest case, a simple loop program with interrupt support can work. Both the Arduino and the Raspberry Pi, mentioned here, are based on the ARM architecture.

The 32-bit implementation of the Arduino architecture is a strong candidate for Cubesat onboard computers. Many implementations feature a real-time clock, which is an add-on item in the Raspberry Pi architecture. A real time clock allows for the implementation of a real-time operating system. Cubesats with Arduinos have flown in orbit. The Arduino mini on the unit from Interorbital systems incorporates a current sensor to indicate a single event upset may have occurred due to radiation. The Arduino architecture has a relatively low tolerance to radiation damage.

Although the Raspberry Pi is not designed to be Rad hard, it showed a surprisingly good radiation tolerance in tests. It continued to operate through a dose of 150 krad(Si), with only the loss of USB connectivity. Several commercial cubesat flight computers are based on the ARM architecture of the Pi.

The NanoMind A712D is an onboard computer for Cubesats. It uses as 32-bit ARM cpu, with 2 megabytes of RAM, and 8 megabytes of flash memory. It can also support a MicroSD flash card. It has a Can bus and a I^2C interface. It comes with an extensive software library and real time operating system. Special applications, such as attitude determination and control code are available. It is tolerant to temperatures form -40 to 85 degrees C, but is not completely rad-hard.

The UK Space agency kicked off a project in December of 2014 called Astro Pi. It was a competition for primary and secondary schools to come up with a project and associated code for a Cubesat. Two units were taken by British Astronaut Tim Peake to the International Space Station in December of 2015. Each has a camera (one for visible spectrum, one for infrared), and each has a magnetometer as well as temperature and humidity sensors. Each unit is standard, but is housed in a purpose built aluminum case.

ARM Simulation and Hardware Debug

The ARM Instruction Set Simulator, ARMulator, is a software development and debug tool provided by ARM Ltd to users of ARM-based chips. Now dated, it is still a good basic tool for system development and debug.

The ARMulator required more than a 1 million lines of C code. It is more than just an instruction set simulator, also providing a virtual platform for system emulation. It can emulate an ARM processor and certain ARM coprocessors. If the processor is part of an embedded system, licensees are allowed to extend ARMulator to add specific implementations of the additional hardware to the ARMulator model. ARMulator supports time-based behavior and event scheduling. ARMulator includes examples of memory-mapped and co-processor expansions. ARMulator can be used to emulate the entire embedded system. ARMulator can be used to simulate a single ARM CPU at one time, although almost all ARM cores up to ARM11 are available.

ARMulator allows runtime debugging using either ARM-sd (ARM Symbolic Debugger), or either of the graphical debuggers that were shipped in SDT and the later ADS products. It was available on a very broad range of platforms including Mac, RISC OS platforms, DEC Alpha, HP-UX, Solaris, SunOS, Windows, GNU/linux.

ARMulator-II formed the basis for the high accuracy, cycle-callable co-verification models of ARM processors, these CoVs models were the basis of many CoVerification systems for ARM processors.

Special models were produced during the development of CPUs, notably the ARM9E, ARM10 and ARM11, these models helped with architectural decisions such as Thumb-2 and TrustZone. ARMulator has been replaced by Just-in-Time compilation-based high performance CPU and system models.

ARMulator I was released in open source and is the basis for the GNU version of ARMulator. Key differences are in the memory interface and services The GNU ARMulator is available as part of the GDB debugger in the ARM GNU Tools.

Hardware debug support is built into the ARM architecture. This allows visibility and access to all registers and memory contents. A serial wire debug port and JTAG support allows visibility of processor internals. Serial wire debug uses a simplified JTAG interface. Data watchpoints and instruction traces are supported in the ARM Debug Interface Specification.

Keil provides a range of Debug and Trace support tools for the ARM architecture as well. Other vendors include WindRiver, Greenhills, and Mentor Graphics

Asynchronous ARM

Like most processors, the ARM is a synchronous digital design, meaning it is clock-driven. An asynchronous version of the ARM was designed in 1990-2000 as an exercise to research the power reduction possible with this technique. It was called the Amulet1 by the APT Group. There are cooperating concurrent units, and a synchronous section of the design. An Occam model was derived, called *OccARM*. The Occam programming language provides the conceptual framework, and the tools for programming parallelism. Superscalar machines exploit independent execution of multiple execution units to achieve a low level parallelism, and break the one instruction per clock limit per package. Certain classes of problems decompose easily into autonomous subtasks for simultaneous execution. An earlier instantiation of the Cooperating Synchronous Processes (CSP's) of the Occam language was the Inmos Transputer. The language came first, then the implementation in hardware. In this sense, it was like Java.

Asynchronous designs introduce non-deterministic behavior, and this makes them hard to test. The architecture also presents a major challenge for optimizing compiler design, and applications in real-time systems.

The Amulet1 achieved about a 70% ARM6 performance with a comparable power consumption. The functionality was demonstrated, and subsequent units showed a reduction in power usage. The work is being pursued under the European Open Microprocessor Initiative.

Appendix – Memory management

The memory management unit (MMU) is an integral part of most processors, and maps virtual addresses to physical addresses. The virtual address space is much large than the physical space. There is an overhead involved with the mapping process, but having transparent access to a large amount of memory is usually an overriding advantage.

Virtual memory is an abstraction. We pretend we have more memory than is available in the system, but we only see a portion of this memory at a given time. The contents of the physical memory that we do have are managed by hardware, and are swapped in and out from secondary storage. Data is transferred in blocks. The program can be written without worrying about how much memory is available. Actually, if we add more physical memory, the systems will run faster, because fewer swaps are required.

Memory management allows a program to run anywhere in memory without being recompiled. It provides a level of protection and isolation between programs to prevent overwriting. It removes restrictions on the size of available memory by the virtual memory technique.

A memory management unit (MMU) translates memory addresses from logical/virtual to physical. This adds the overhead of translation to each memory access. In addition, the access time for the secondary storage may be a million times slower than for the primary memory, but it will have 100's of times large capacity, and certainly be cheaper. There is also the energy consumption issue.

When the CPU accesses a desired item, it may be present in the memory, or not. If not, the process generates a Page fault, resulting in an interrupt, with a request for data item not currently resident. This requires clever programming to be an efficient process. Too many misses, and the process bogs down in overhead.

The scheme requires data structures to keep track of what range of data addresses is actually present in memory, and registers or tables to allow arbitrary mappings of logical to physical addresses.

There are two basic schemes: segmented and paged. Paged usually deals with fixed sized blocks of memory, and segmentation is more flexible in terms of size. Segmentation and paging can be combined in certain architectures.

One application of memory mapping, often overlooked, is that the mapping process can map around failed physical memory, by moving pointers. It there is an active memory error detection and correction scheme running in hardware (or software), the mapping tables can be used to move code or data out of problem areas in the physical memory, without changing the associated program (or data) address.

Appendix - Input/Output

This sections discusses and provides background on basic computer I/O operations. There is nothing ARM-specific here. Input/Output (I/O) provides a user interface, and a link between systems. The basic I/O methods of polled, interrupt, and dma are supported by the CPU chips, but additional support chips are required to implement these functions. There are many options. We will consider the specific implementation of the IBM pc circuit board, which has evolved into an industry standard architecture.

I/O Methods

Regardless how bits or signals come to a computer, there are several standards methods to sample them, or send them out. The various communication protocols define the physical connection (connectors) and electrical interface (voltages, etc.). Once we are at the processor chip boundary, and we are dealing with bits, there are three common schemes to read or write. These can be implemented in hardware or software. The three schemes are polled I/O, interrupts, or direct memory access. All of these schemes work with serial (bit-at-a-time) or parallel (many-bits-at-a-time) I/O. There are three basic methods for I/O implementation, polled I/O, interrupts, and direct memory access.

Polled I/O

In polled I/O, the computer periodically checks to see if data is available, or if the communications channel is ready to accept new output. This is somewhat like checking your phone every few seconds to see if anyone is calling. There's a more efficient way to do it, which we'll discuss next, but you may not have anything better to do. Polled I/O is the simplest method. Specific I/O instructions are provided in the Intel processors. Both serial and parallel interfaces are used on the IBM pc board level architecture.

Interrupt

In Interrupt I/O, when a new piece of information arrives, or the communication channel is ready to accept new output, a control signal called an interrupt occurs. This is like the phone ringing. You are sitting at your desk, busy at something, and the phone rings, interrupting you, causing you to set aside what you are doing, and handle the new task. When that is done, you go back to what you were doing. A special piece of software called an interrupt service routine is required. At this point, the phone rings….

Control transfer mechanism, somewhat like a subroutine call, but can be triggered by an external event. External events can make a request for service. The Intel CPU architecture supports 256 levels of interrupt, with a single interrupt line. The specific interrupt number is put on the CPU data bus, in the lower 8-bits. This requires one or more external interrupt prioritization chips. The IBM pc architecture uses 8 levels of interrupt, and the later IBM AT architecture supports 15.

Sources for Interrupts

There are hardware interrupts, defined by the architecture of the CPU and the motherboard it resides on. These interrupts are triggered by events external to the CPU, and are thus asynchronous to its operation

We can get the same effect by executing software interrupt commands. This provides a convenient mechanism for a user program to call the Operating System and request services. There interrupts are synchronous.

Exceptions are interrupts caused in response to a condition encountered during execution of an instruction. For example, an attempted division by zero would trigger an exception. These are also synchronous interrupts.

External Interrupts are asynchronous to the CPU's operation. It is hard to duplicate their timing. There are implications for debugging multiple interrupt systems in a real-time environment. We need to know the state of the machine, at every instant of time.

DMA

Direct Memory access is the fastest way to input or output information. It does this directly to or from memory, without processor intervention.

Let's say we want to transmit a series of 32-bit words. The processor would have to fetch this word from memory, send it to the I/O interface, and update a counter. In DMA, the I/O device can interface directly to or from the memory. DMA control hardware includes housekeeping tasks such as keeping a word count, and updating the memory pointer.

DMA also makes use of interrupts. Normally, we load a word count into a register in the DMA controller, and it is counted down as words transfer to or from memory. When the word count reaches zero, and interrupt is triggered to the processor to signal the end of the transfer event.

While the DMA is going on, the processor may be locked out of memory access, depending on the memory architecture. Also, if dynamic memory is being used, the processor is usually in charge of memory refresh. This can be handled by the DMA controller, but someone has to do it.

The DMA scheme used on the IBM pc toggles between the CPU and the DMA device on a per-word basis. Thus, the processor is not locked out of fetching and executing instructions during a DMA, although the DMA transfer is not as fast as it could be.

Also, DMA is not constrained to access memory linearly; that is a function of the DMA controller and its complexity. For example, the DMA controller can be set up to access every fourth word in memory.

The DMA protocol uses a Request and Grant mechanism. The device desiring to use dma send a request to the CPU, and that request is granted when the CPU is able. This is similar to the interrupt request for service mechanism. A dma controller interfaces with the device and the CPU. It may handle multiple dma channels with differing priorities. The controller has to know, for each request, the starting address in memory, and the size of the data movement. For dma data coming in to ram, there is the additional complication of updating cache.

During the DMA transfer, the dma controller takes over certain tasks from the CPU. This includes updating the memory address, and keeping track of the word count. The word count normally goes to zero, and generates an interrupt to signal the CPU that the DMA transfer is over. The CPU can continue execution, as long as it has code and data available.

Serial versus parallel

A bus architecture is used as a short-distance parallel communications pathway between functional elements, such as the CPU and memory. The length of parallel signal lines is severely restricted by bit skew, where all the bits don't get to a particular point at the same time. This is due in some part by the differing characteristics of the circuit board traces implementing the bus. Each path must be treated as a transmission line at the frequencies involved, and have balanced characteristics with all the other lines, and be properly terminated.

Serial communication can take place at gigabit rates, and does not suffer from bit skew. In addition, it can take be used over arbitrary distances, and with various carrier schemes. At this moment, the Voyager spacecraft is sending data back to Earth over a serial radio frequency link, even though the spacecraft is outside the solar system, at a nominal 40 bits per second.

A UART, Universal Asynchronous Receiver Transmitter, has industry standard functionality for serial asynchronous communication. An example of the hardware part is the 8251 chip. A UART may also be implemented in software. The functionality includes support for all of the standard formats (bits, parity, and overhead).

Serial communication of multiple bits utilizes time domain multiplexing of the communication channel, as bits are transmitted one at a time.

The serial communication parameters of interest include:
- Baud rate. (Symbol rate)
- Number of bits per character.
- endian – MSB or LSB transmitted first
- Parity/no parity.
- If parity, even or odd.
- Length of a stop bit (1, 1.5, 2 bits)

The baud rate gives the speed of transmission of data characters. The bit rate is the speed of individual bits making up the information and the overhead. For example, if we have 8 data bits and 3 overhead bits, and we transfer characters at 1000 baud, we are using a bit rate of 13000 bits per second.

What is the length of a bit? This is the time period of a bit, the reciprocal of the frequency. At 1000 Hertz, a bit is 1/1000 second, or 1 millisecond long.

In synchronous communication, a shared clock is used between the transmitter and receiver. This clock can be transmitted on a second channel, or be a shared resource, such as GPS-derived time. In synchronous systems, characters are transmitted continuously. If there is no data to transmit, a special SYN character is used.

In asynchronous communication, the transmitter and receiver have their own local clocks, and the receiver must synchronize to the transmitter clock. The receiver and transmitter clocks are usually very accurate, being derived from crystal oscillators. Clock drift between the units is less of a problem than phase – the receiver does not know when a transmission begins. This is accomplished by a shared protocol.

When characters are not being transmitted in an asynchronous scheme, the communications channel is kept at a known idle state, known as a "Mark", from the old time telegraph days. Morse code is binary, and the manual teletypes used the presence or absence of a voltage (or current through the line) to represent one state, and the absence to indicate the other state. Initially, the key press or "1" state was "voltage is applied", and the resting state was no voltage. Since these early systems used acid-filled batteries, there was a desire among operators to extend the battery life, without having to refill the batteries. Problem is, if the wire were cut (maliciously or accidentally), there was no indication. The scheme was changed to where the resting state was voltage on the line. Thus, if the line voltage dropped to zero, there was a problem on the channel.

The digital circuitry uses mostly 5 volts, and the RS-232 standard for serial communication specifies a plus/minus voltage. Usually 12 volts works fine. In any case, interface circuitry at each end of the line convert line voltage to +5/0 volts for the computer circuitry. One state is called "marking" and the other state is called "spacing".

The receiver does bit re-timing on what it receives. Knowing when the transmission started, and the width of the bits, it knows when to sample them and make a choice between one and zero. From communications theory, the best place to sample is in the middle of the bit.

At idle, which is an arbitrary period in asynchronous communication, the input assumes one known state. When it changes to another state, the receiver knows this is the start of a transmission, and the beginning or leading edge of a "start" bit. Since the receiver knows the baud rate a priori, because of an agreement with the transmitter, it waits one bit period to get to the first data bit leading edge, and then an additional one-half bit period to get to the middle of the bit. This is the ideal point (in communications theory terms) to sample the input bit. After, that, the receiver waits one additional bit period to sample the second bit in the center, etc., for the agreed-upon number of bits in a word. Then the receiver samples the parity bit (if the agreement allows for one), and then waits one, one and a half, or two bit periods for the "stop bits". After that, any change in the sensed bit state is the start bit of a new transmission. If the receiver and transmitter use different baud clock, the received data will not be sensed at the right time, and will be incorrect. If the format is incorrect, if the receiver expects eight data bits, and the transmitter sends seven, the received word will be incorrect. This may or may not be caught by the parity bit.

Can the receiver derive clock information from the data stream, without prior knowledge of the baud rate? Yes, if special characters (sync words) are sent first. The format has to be agreed-upon. When the receiver sees a state transition on the line, it takes this to mean the leading edge of the start bit. It starts a local timer, and stops the timer, when the line state changes. This means the first data bit has to have the opposite state from a start bit. The receiver now knows the width of a bit, and divides this by two and start sampling the data bits in the middle..

If special characters are used, the receiver can guess the format of the data format to a good degree of accuracy. Given the initial guess, the receiver can transmit a request byte back to the original transmitter for a specific character, which then nails down the format. Note that this is not generally implemented in hardware UARTS, but can be accomplished in software.

In full duplex systems, data can be sent and received simultaneously over the link. This means the communications link has to have twice the capacity of a half-duplex link, which only allows the transmission of data in one direction at a time. Each link has a practical maximum rate of transmission, which is called the communication channel capacity. It is the upper bound to the amount of information that can be successfully transferred on the channel. That depends on noise, which corrupts the received information. Claude Shannon derived the concept of channel capacity, and provided an equation to calculate it. It is related to the signal to noise ratio of the channel.

In a Master/Slave system, one device is master and others are slaves. The master can initiate messages to individual slave units. This scheme is typically used in bus systems. The master can also broadcast a message to all units. In a Multi-Master scheme there is more than one master, and an arbitration scheme is necessary. This usually is implemented with a protocol for other devices than the current master to request bus mastership, which is then granted when feasible or convenient.

In a Peer-Peer scheme, on the other hand, there is no master, everyone is equal. This is the scheme used for Ethernet. If two units transmit at the same time, the transmission is garbled, and each unit retries after a random wait. If the randomness scheme works, this scheme is highly effective.

Baud rate generation is handled locally at a transmitter or receiver by a crystal oscillator. It is usually 16 times the bit rate, to provide adequate sampling of the incoming signal for receivers. It can be selected to several values. The sample clock can be different on the receiver and transmitter, but the baud rate must be the same.

Parity is a simple error control mechanism for communications and storage. We add an extra bit to the word, so we can adjust parity. Parity is based on the mathematical concept of even (evenly divisible by two) or odd. In binary, a number is even if its least-significant (rightmost) digit is zero (0).

For example, in ASCII,

A = 4116 = 0100 0001 2 (1's) = even
B = 4216 = 0100 0010 2 (1's) = even
C = 4316 = 0100 0011 3 (1's) = odd

If we want to always have even parity, we would make the extra bit = 0 for A & B, 1 for C, etc.

If we want to get fancy, there are other schemes that use multiple bits to allow detection, and even correction, of multiple bit errors.

Appendix – non-integer data formats

Floating Point

This section describes the floating point number representation, and explains when it is used, and why. This is not an ARM-specific section. Floating point is an old computer technique for gaining dynamic range in scientific and engineering calculations, at the cost of accuracy. First, we look at fixed point, or integer, calculations to see where the limitations are. Then, we'll examine how floating point helps expand the limits.

In a finite word length machine, there is a tradeoff between dynamic range and accuracy in representation. The value of the most significant bit sets the dynamic range because the effective value of the most positive number is infinity. The value of the least significant bit sets the accuracy, because a value less than the LSB is zero. And, the MSB and the LSB are related by the word length.

In any fixed point machine, the number system is of a finite size. For example, in 18 bit word, we can represent the positive integers from 0 to $2^{18}-1$, or 262,143. A word of all zeros = 0, and a word of all ones = 262,143. I'm using 18 bits as an example because it's not too common. There's nothing magic about 8, 16, or 32 bit word sizes.

If we want to use signed numbers, we must give up one bit to represent the sign. Of course, giving up one bit halves the number of values available in the representation. For a signed integer in an 18 bit word, we can represent integers from + to - 131,072. Of course, zero is a valid number. Either the positive range or the negative range must give up a digit so we can represent zero. For now, let's say that in 18 bits, we can represent the integers from -131,072 to 131,071.

There are several ways of using the sign bit for representation. We can have a sign-magnitude format, a 1's complement, or a two's complement representation. Most computers use the 2's complement representation. This is easy to implement in hardware. In this format, to form the negative of a number, complement all of the bits (1->0, 0->1), and add 1 to the least significant bit position. This is equivalent to forming the 1's complement, and then adding one. One's complement format has the problem that there are two representations of zero, all bits 0 and all bits 1. The hardware has to know that these are equivalent. This added complexity has led to 1's complement schemes falling out of use in favor of 2's complement. In two's complement, there is one representation of zero (all bits zero), and one less positive number, than the negatives. (Actually, since zero is considered positive, there are the same number. But, the negative numbers have more range.) This is easily illustrated for 3 bit numbers, and can be extrapolated to any other fixed length representation.

Remember that the difference between a signed and an unsigned number lies in our interpretation of the bit pattern.

Interpretation of 4-bit patterns

Up to this point we have considered the bit patterns to represent integer values, but we can also insert an arbitrary binary point (analogous to the decimal point) in the word. For integer representations, we have assumed the binary point to lie at the right side of the word, below the LSB. This gives the LSB a weight of 2^0, or 1, and the msb has a weight of 2^{16}. (The sign bit is in the 2^{17} position). Similarly, we can use a fractional representation where the binary point is assumed to lie between the sign bit and the MSB, the MSB has a weight of 2^{-1}, and the LSB has a weight of 2^{-17}. For these two cases we have:

The MSB sets the range, the LSB sets the accuracy, and the LSB and MSB are related by the word length. For cases between these extremes, the binary point can lie anywhere in the word, or for that matter, outside the word. For example, if the binary point is assumed to lie 2 bits to the right of the LSB, the LSB weight, and thus the precision, is 2^2. The MSB is then 2^{19}. We have gained dynamic range at the cost of precision. If we assume the binary point is to the left of the MSB, we must be careful to ignore the sign, which does not have an associated digit weight. For an assumed binary point 2 bit positions to the right of the MSB, we have a MSB weight of 2^{-3}, and an LSB weight of 2^{-20}. We have gained precision at the cost of dynamic range.

It is important to remember that the computer does not care where we assume the binary point to be. It simply treats the numbers as integers during calculations. We overlay the bit weights and the meanings.

A 16-bit integer can represent the values between -16384 to 16384

A 32-bit integer can represent the values between $-2*10^9$ to $2*10^9$

A short real number has the range 10^{-37} to 10^{38} in 32 bits.

A long real number has the range 10^{-307} to 10^{308} in 64 bits

We can get 18 decimal (BCD) digits packed into 80 bits.

To add or subtract scaled values, they must have the same scaling factor; they must be commensurate. If the larger number is normalized, the smaller number must be shifted to align it for the operation. This may have the net result of adding or subtracting zero, as bits fall out the right side of the small word. This is like saying that 10 billion + .00001 is approximately 10 billion, to 13 decimal places of accuracy.

In multiplication, the scaling factor of the result is the sum of the scaling factors of the products. This is analogous to engineering notation, where we learn to add the powers of 10.

In division, the scaling factor of the result is the difference between the scaling factor of the dividend and the scaling factor of the divisor. The scaling factor of the remainder is that of the dividend. In engineering notation, we subtract the powers of 10 for a division.

In a normal form for a signed integer, the most significant bit is one. This says, in essence, that all leading zeros have been squeezed out of the number. The sign bit does not take part in this procedure. However, note that if we know that the most significant bit is always a one, there is no reason to store it. This gives us a free bit in a sense; the most significant bit is a 1 by definition, and the msb-1 th bit is adjacent to the sign bit. This simple trick has doubled the effective accuracy of the word, because each bit position is a factor of two.

The primary operation that will cause a loss of precision or accuracy is the subtraction of two numbers that have nearly but not quite identical values. This is commonly encountered in digital filters, for example, where successive readings are differenced. For an 18 bit word, if the readings differ in, say, the 19th bit position, then the difference will be seen to be zero. On the other hand, the scaling factor of the parameters must allow sufficient range to hold the largest number expected. Care must be taken in subtracting values known to be nearly identical. Precision can be retained by pre-normalization of the arguments.

During an arithmetic operation, if the result is a value larger than the greatest positive value for a particular format, or less than the most negative, then the operation has overflowed the format. Normally, the absolute value function cannot overflow, with the exception of the absolute value of the least negative number, which has no corresponding positive representation, because we made room for the representation of zero.

In addition, the scaling factor can increase by one, if we consider the possibility of adding two of the largest possible numbers. We can also consider subtracting the largest (absolute value) negative number from the largest (in an absolute sense) negative number.

A one bit position left shift is equivalent to multiplying by two. Thus, after a one position shift, the scaling factor must be adjusted to reflect the new position of the binary point. Similarly, a one bit position right shift is equivalent to division by two, and the scaling factor must be similarly adjusted after the operation.

Numeric overflow occurs when a nonzero result of an arithmetic operation is too small in absolute value to be represented. The result is usually reported as zero. The subtraction case discussed above is one example. Taking the reciprocal of the largest positive number is another.

As in the decimal representation, some numbers cannot be represented exactly in binary, regardless of the precision. Non-terminating fractions such as 1/3 are one case, and the irrational numbers such as e and pi are another. Operations involving these will result in inexact results, regardless of the format. However, this is not necessarily an error. The irrationals, by definition, cannot exactly be represented by a ratio of integers. Even in base 10 notation, e and pi extend indefinitely.

When the results of a calculation do not fix within the format, we must throw something away. We normally delete bits from the right (or low side) side of the word (the precision end). There are several ways to do this. If we simply ignore the bits that won't fit within the format, we are truncating, or rounding toward zero. We choose the closest word within the format to represent the results. We can also round up by adding 1 to the LSB of the resultant word if the first bit we're going to throw away is a 1. We can also choose to round to even, round to odd, round to nearest, round towards zero, round towards + infinity, or round towards - infinity. Consistency is the desired feature.

If we look at typical physical constants, we can get some idea of the dynamic range that we'll require for typical applications. The mass of an electron, you recall, is 9.1085×10^{-31} grams. Avogadro's number is 6.023×10^{23}. If we want to multiply these quantities, we need a dynamic range of $10^{(23+31)} = 10^{54}$, which would require a 180 bit word (10^{54} approx.$= 2^{180}$). Most of the bits in this 180 bit word would be zeros as place holders. Well, since zeros don't mean anything, can't we get rid of them? Of course.

We need dynamic range, and we need precision, but we usually don't need them simultaneously. The floating point data structure will give us dynamic range, at the cost of being unable to exactly represent data.

So, finally, we talk about floating point. In essence, we need a format for the computer to work with that is analogous to engineering notation, a mantissa and a power of ten. The two parts of the word, with their associated signs, will take part in calculation exactly like the scaled integers discussed previously. The exponent is the scaling factor that we used. Whereas in scaled integers, we had a fixed scaling factor, in floating point, we allow the scaling factor to be carried along with the word, and to change as the calculations proceed.

The representation of a number in floating point, like the representation in scientific notation, is not unique. For example,

$$6.54 \times 10^2 = .654 \times 10^3 = 654. \times 10^0$$

We have to choose a scheme and be consistent. What is normally done is that the exponent is defined to be a number such that the leftmost digit is non-zero. This is defined as the normal form.

In the floating point representation, the number of bits assigned to the exponent determines dynamic range, and the number of bits assigned to the mantissa determine the precision, or resolution. For a fixed word size, we must allocate the available bits between the precision (mantissa), and the range (exponent).

Granularity is defined as the difference between representable numbers. This term is normally equal to the absolute precision, and relates to the least significant bit.

Denormalized numbers

This topic is getting well into the number of theory, and I will only touch on these special topics here. There is a use for numbers that are not in normal form, so-called de-normals. This has to do with decreasing granularity, and the fact that numbers in the range between zero and the smallest normal number. A denorm has an exponent which is the smallest representable exponent, with a leading digit of the mantissa not equal to zero. An un-normalized number, on the other hand, has the same mantissa case, but an exponent which is not the smallest representable. Let's get back to engineering...

Overflow and Underflow

If the result of an operation results in a number too large (in an absolute magnitude case) to be represented, we have generated an overflow. If the result is too small to be represented, we have an underflow. Results of an overflow can be reported as infinity (+ or - as required), or as an error bit pattern. The underflow case is where we have generated a denormalized number. The IEEE standard, discussed below, handles denorms as valid operands. Another approach is to specify resultant denorms as zero.

Standards

There are many standards for the floating point representation, with the IEEE standard being the defacto industry choice. In this section, we'll discuss the

IEEE standard in detail, and see how some other industry standards differ, and how conversions can be made.

IEEE floating point

The IEEE standard specifies the representation of a number as +/- mantissa x $2^{(+/-\ exponent)}$. Note that there are two sign bits, one for the mantissa, and one for the exponent. Note also that the exponent is an exponent of two, not ten. This is referred to as radix-2 representation. Other radices are possible. The most significant bit of the mantissa is assumed to be a 1, and is not stored. Take a look at what this representation buys us. A 16 bit integer can cover a range of +/- 10^4. A 32 bit integer can span a range of +/- 10^9. The IEEE short real format, in 32 bits, can cover a range of +/- $10^{+/-38}$. A 64 bit integer covers the range +/- 10^{19}. A long real IEEE floating point number covers the range +/- $10^{+/-\ 308}$. The dynamic range of calculations has been vastly increased for the same data size. What we have lost is the ability to exactly represent numbers, but we are close enough for engineering.

In the short, real format, the 32 bit word is broken up into fields. The mantissa, defined as a number less than 1, occupies 23 bits. The most significant bit of the data item is the sign of the mantissa. The exponent occupies 8 bits. The represented word is as follows:

$(-1)^S$ (2^{E+bias}) (F1...F23)

where F0...F23 < 1. Note that F0=1 by definition, and is not stored.

The term $(-1)^S$ gives us + when the S bit is 0 and - when the S bit is 1. The bias term is defined as 127. This is used instead of a sign bit for the exponent, and achieves the same results. This format simplifies the hardware, because only positive numbers are then involved in exponent calculations. As a side benefit, this approach ensures that reciprocals of all representable numbers can be represented.

In the long real format, the structure is as follows:

$(-1)^S$ (2^{E+bias}) (F1...F52)

where F0...F52 < 1. Note that F0=1 by definition, and is not stored.

Here, the bias term is defined as 1023.

For intermediate steps in a calculation, there is a temporary real data format in 80 bits. This expands the exponent to 15 bits, and the mantissa to 64 bits. This allows a range of +/- 10^{4932}, which is a large number in anyone's view.

In the IEEE format, provision is made for entities known as Not-A-Number (NaN). For sample, the result of trying to multiply zero times infinity is NaN. These entities are status signals that particular violation cases took place. IEEE representation also supports four user selectable rounding modes. What do we do with results that won't fit in the bits allocated? Do we round or truncate? If we round, is it towards +/- infinity, or zero? Not all implementations of the IEEE standard implement all of the modes and options.

Floating point hardware is specialized, optimized computer architecture for the floating point data structure. It usually features concurrent operation with host, or the integer unit. Initially, floating point units were separate chips, but now the state of the art allows these functional units to be included on the same silicon real estate as the integer processor. The hardware of the floating point unit is specialized to handle the floating point data format. For example, in a floating multiply, we simultaneously integer multiply the mantissas and add the exponents. A barrel shifter is handy for normalization/renormalization by providing a shift of any number of bits in one clock period. Floating point units usually implement the format conversions in hardware (integer to floating, float,; floating to integer, Fix), and can handle extended precision (64 bit) integers. Both external and internal floating point units usually rely on the main processor's instruction fetch unit. The coprocessor may have to do a memory access for load/store. In this case, it may use a dma-like protocol to get use of the memory bus resource from the integer processor.

Floating point hardware gives us the ability to add, subtract, multiply, and sometimes divide. Some units provide only the reciprocal function, which is a simple divide into a known fixed quantity (1), and thus easy to implement. A divide requires two operations, then, a reciprocal followed by a multiply. Some units also include square root, and some transcendental primitives. In general, these functions are implemented in a microstep fashion, with Taylor or other series expansions of the functions of interest.

signed integer range $2 \wedge (\text{bits} - 1)$

10 bits 1 x 10^3 (a good approximation is 2^{10} is approx. 10^3)

16 bits 3 x 10^4

32 bits 2 x 10^9

64 bits 9.2 x 10^{18}

128 bits 1.7 x 10^{38}

256 bits 1.1 x 10^{77}

Floating Point operations

This subsection discuses operations on floating point numbers. This forms the basis for the specification of a floating point emulation software package, or for the development of custom hardware.

Before the addition can be performed, the floating point numbers must be commensurate with addition; in essence, they must have the same exponent. The mantissa of the number with the smaller exponent will be right shifted, and the exponent adjusted accordingly. However, if the right shift is equal to or more than the number of bits in the mantissa representation, we will lose something. This is analogous to the case where we add 0.000001 to 1 million and get approximately 1 million.

After the addition of mantissas, we may need to right shift the resultant by 1, and adjust the exponent accordingly, to account for mantissa overflow. This is analogous to the case of adding 4.1 x 10^{16} + 6.3 x 10^{16}, with the result of 10.4 x 10^{16}, or 1.04 * 10^{17}, in normal form.

If we add two numbers of almost equal magnitude but opposite sign, we get a case of massive cancellation. Here, the leading digits of the mantissa may be zero, with a loss of precision. Renormalization is always called for after addition.

example: 1.23456 * 10^{16} plus -1.23455 * 10^{16} = 0.00001 x 10^{16}, or 1.0 * 10^{11}, in normal form.

In multiply, we may simultaneously multiply the mantissas, and add the exponents. After the operation, we need to renormalize the results. In division, we divide the mantissas and subtract the exponents, then renormalize.

84

The easiest division to do is a reciprocal, where the dividend is a known quantity. Some systems implement only the reciprocal operation, requiring a following multiplication to complete the division operation. Even so, this may be faster than a division, because the reciprocal is much easier to implement in algorithmic form than the general purpose division.

Transcendentals

The floating point unit can also implement transcendental functions. These are usually Taylor series expansions of common trigonometric and log functions. Enough transcendentals are included to provide basis functions for all we might need to calculate.

- F2XM1 - 2X-1
- FYL2X - Y * log2 (X)
- FYL2XP1 - Y * log2(X+1)
- FPTAN - tangent
- FPATAN - arctangent

From the basis functions, if x=tan(a), then a = atan (x), then

- $sin(a) = x / sqrt(1 + x2)$
- $cos(a) = 1 / sqrt (1 + x2)$
- $asin(x) = atan[x/sqrt(1-x2)]$

There are known functions to calculate 2^x, e^x, 10^x, and y^x in terms of the F2MX1 (2^x-1) function. Similarly, the log base e and base 10 can be calculated in terms of the FYL2X (log base 2) function. All of the trigonometric, inverse trigonometric, hyperbolic, and inverse hyperbolic functions can be calculated in terms of the supplied basis functions.

Graphics Processing Unit (GPU)

A GPU is a specialized computer architecture to manipulate image data at high rates. It can be a single chip, or incorporated with a general purpose CPU. The GPU devices are highly parallel, and specifically designed to handle image data, and operations on that data. They do this much fastest than a programmed general purpose CPU. Most desktop machines have the GPU function on a video card or integrated with their CPU. Originally, GPU's were circuit card based. GPU operations are very memory intensive. The GPU design is customized to (Single Instruction, Multiple Data) SIMD type operations.

The instruction set of the GPU is specific to graphics operations on block data. The requirements were driven by the demands of 2-D and 3-D video games on pc's, phones, tablets, and dedicated gaming units. As GPU units became faster and more capable, they began to consume more power (and thus generate more heat) than the associated CPU's. They are applicable to many classes of Science Data processing.

Although designed to process video data, some GPU's have been used as adjunct data processors and accelerators in other areas involving vectors and matrices, such as the inverse discrete cosine transform. Types of higher-level processing implemented by GPU's include texture mapping, polygon rendering, object rotation, and coordination system transformation. They also support object shading operations, data oversampling, and interpolation. GPU's find a major application area in video decoding. Building on this, GPU's enable advanced features in digital cameras. These features are supported by Image Processing Libraries. This can be employed in star-tracking cameras, and to facilitate orbit and attitude calculations.

Vector Processor

Vector processing involves the processing of vectors of related data, in a (single instruction, multiple data) *SIMD* mode. For example, vector addition is an SIMD operation.

SIMD refers to a class of parallel computers that perform the same operations on multiple data items simultaneously. This is data level parallelism, which is found in multimedia (video and audio) data used in gaming applications. The SIMD approach evolved from the vector supercomputers of the 1970's, which operated upon a vector of data with a single operation. Sun Microsystems introduced SIMD operations in their SPARC architecture in 1995. A popular application of SIMD architecture is Intel's MMX (Multimedia Extensions) instruction set circa 1996 for the X-86 architecture.

Digital Signal Processor

Digital signal processors resemble computers in many ways, and come in embedded versions. They handle specialized data types, and include special-purpose operations derived from the digital signal processing realm. This includes the Multiply-and-Add (mac), a digital filtering primitive. Digital signal processing finds application with the processing of audio and video data.

A Digital Signal Processor (DSP) is similar to a general purpose CPU, but provides specialized operations for DSP-type operations on specialized data formats. Originally, the DSP function was implemented by software running in a CPU. DSP operations usually have time deadline constraints (hard real time requirements).

Mobile phones and cable modems, to name two examples, drove the development of faster, dedicated hardware units. The first practical commercial product based on a DSP chip was Texas Instrument's Speak-n-

Spell toy. Before that, the military applications of sonar and radar data processing drove the technology.

The nature of digital domain signal data and filtering require some unique architectural features. Hardware modulo addressing and bit-reversed addressing is used in digital filtering. Operations on data tend to be SIMD. The *Multiply-Accumulate* primitive is the basis for digital filter implementation. Saturation arithmetic is used to prevent overflow. Both fixed point and floating point data are used. A three-memory Harvard architecture allows simultaneous access of an opcode and two operands.
Multicore chips for DSP are now common. These fast DSP's have enabled new technologies and applications such as software-defined radio.

An illustrative device is Analog Devices' Blackfin series of embedded DSP's. These chips are supported by a real-time operating systems. The Blackfin is a 32-bit RISC processor with dual 16-bit multiply/accumulate (MAC) units, and provision for 8-bit video processing in real-time.

ARM chips such as the Cortex-8 family, and the OMAP3 processors include both a general purpose CPU, and a DSP.

Appendix – Cache

This section discusses the concept of a cache in generic computer architecture terms. A cache is a temporary memory buffer for data. It is placed between the processor and the main memory. The cache is smaller, but faster than the main memory. Being faster, it is more expensive, so it serves as a transition to the main store. They may be several levels of cache (L1, L2, L3), the one closest to the processor having the highest speed, commensurate to the processor. That closest to the main memory has a lower speed, but is still faster than the main memory. The cache has faster access times, and becomes valuable when items are accessed multiple times. Cache is transparent to the user; it has no specific address.

There can be different caches for instructions and data, or a unified cache for both. Code is usually accessed in linear fashion, but data items are not. In a running program, the code cache is never written, simplifying its design. The nature of accessing for instructions and data is different. On a read access, if the desired item is present in a cache, we get a cache hit, and the item is read. If the item is not in cache, we get a cache miss, and the item must be fetched from memory. There is a small additional time penalty in this process over going directly to memory (in the case of a miss). Cache works because, on the average, we will have the desired item in cache most of the time, by design.

Cache reduces the average access time for data, but will increase the worst-case time. The size and organization of the cache defines the performance for a given program. The proper size and organization is the subject of much analysis and simulation.

Caches introduce indeterminacy in execution time. With cache, memory access time is no longer deterministic. We can't tell, a priori, if an item is or is not in cache. This can be a problem in some real-time systems.

A working set is a set of memory locations used by a program in a certain time interval. This can refer to code or data. Ideally, the working set is in cache. The cache stores not only the data item, but a tag, which identifies where the item is from in main memory. Advanced systems can mark ranges of items in memory as non-cacheable, meaning they are only used once, and don't need to take up valuable cache space.

For best performance, we want to keep frequently-accessed locations in fast cache. Also, cache retrieves more than one word at a time, it retrieves a "line" of data, which can vary in size. Sequential accesses are faster after an initial access (both in cache and regular memory) because of the overhead of set-up times.

Writing data back to cache does not necessarily get it to main memory right away. With a write-through cache, we do immediately copy the written item to main memory. With a write-back cache, we write to main memory only when a location is removed from the cache.

Many locations can map onto the same cache block. Conflict misses are easy to generate: If array A uses locations 0, 1, 2, ... and array b uses locations 1024, 1025, 1026, ..., the operation a[i] + b[i] generates conflict misses in a cache of size 1024.

Caches, then, provide a level of performance increase at the cost of complexity due to temporal or spatial locality of the data. The program is not aware of the location of the data, whether it is in cache or main memory. The only indication is the run time of the program.

Cache hierarchy

This includes the L1, L2, and L3 caches. L1 is the smallest cache, located closest to the CPU, usually on the same chip. Some CPU have all three levels on chip. Each of the levels of cache is a different size and organization, and has different policies, to optimize performance at that point.

A key parameter of cache is the replacement policy. The replacement policy strategy is for choosing which cache entry to overwrite to make room for a new data. There are two popular strategies: random, and least-recently used

(LRU). In random, we simply choose a location, write the data back to main memory, and refill the cache from the new desired location. In least recently used scenario, the hardware keeps track of cache accesses, and chooses the least recently used item to swap out.

As long as the hardware keeps track of access, it can keep track of writes to the cache line. If the line has not been written into, it is the same as the items in memory, and a write-back operation is not required. The flag that keeps track of whether the cache line has been written into is called the "dirty" bit. This book does discuss the dirty bits of computer architecture.

Note that we are talking about cache as implemented in random access memory of varying speeds. The concept is the same for memory swapped back and forth to rotating disk; what was called virtual memory in mainframes.

Cache organization

In a fully-associative cache, any memory location can be stored anywhere in the cache. This form is almost never implemented. In a direct-mapped cache, each memory location maps onto exactly one cache entry. In an N-way set-associative cache, each memory location can go into one of n sets. Direct mapped cache has the best hit times. Fully associative cache has the lowest miss rates.

TLB

The Translation Lookaside Buffer (TLB) is a cache used to expedite the translation of virtual to physical memory address. It holds pairs of virtual and translated (physical addresses). If the required translation is present (meaning it was done recently), the process is speeded up.

Caches have a direct effect on performance and determinacy, but the system designer does not always have a choice, when the caches are incorporated as part of the CPU. In this case, the system designer needs to review the cache design choices to ensure it is commensurate with the problem being address by the system.

Glossary of System Terms and Acronyms

1's complement – a binary number representation scheme for negative values.

2's complement – another binary number representation scheme for negative values.

2-wire – twisted pair wire channel for full duplex communications. Still needs a common ground.

802.11 – a radio frequency wireless data communications standard.

Accumulator – a register to hold numeric values during and after an operation.

ACM – Association for Computing Machinery; professional organization.

Actuator – device which converts a control signal to a mechanical action.

Ada – a programming language named after Ada Augusta, Countess of Lovelace, and daughter of Lord Byron; arguably, the first programmer. Collaborator with Charles Babbage.

A/D, ADC – analog to digital converter.

ALU – arithmetic logic unit.

Android – an operating system based on Gnu-GNU/linux, popular for smart phones and tablet computers.

Analog – concerned with continuous values.

ANSI – American National Standards Institute

API – application program interface; specification for software modules to communicate.

Arduino – open source, single board microcontroller using an Atmel AVR (8-bit risc) CPU.

Arinc – Aeronautical Radio, Inc. commercial company supporting transportation, and providing standards for avionics.

ARM – Acorn RISC machine; a 32-bit architecture with wide application in embedded systems.

ArpaNet – Advanced Research Projects Agency (U.S.), first packet switched network, 1968.

ASCII - American Standard Code for Information Interchange, a 7-bit code; developed for teleprinters.

ASIC – application specific integrated circuit.

Assembly language – low level programming language specific to a particular ISA.

Async – asynchronous; using different clocks.

Babbage, Charles –early 19th century inventor of mechanical computing machinery to solve difference equations, and output typeset results; later machines would be fully programmable.

Baud – symbol rate; may or may not be the same as bit rate.

Baudot – a five-bit code used with teleprinters.

BCD – binary coded decimal. 4-bit entity used to represent 10 different decimal digits; with 6 spare states.

Beowulf – clustering technology for Gnu-GNU/linux-based computers.

Big-endian – data format with the most significant bit or byte at the lowest address, or transmitted first.

Binary – using base 2 arithmetic for number representation.

BIOS – basic input output system; first software run after boot.

BIST – built-in self test.

Bit – smallest unit of digital information; two states.

Blackbox – functional device with inputs and outputs, but no detail on the internal workings.

Bluetooth – short range open wireless communications standard.

Boolean – a data type with two values; an operation on these data types; named after George Boole, mid-19th century inventor of Boolean algebra.

Bootstrap – a startup or reset process that proceeds without external intervention.

BSD – Berkeley Software Distribution version of the Bell Labs Unix operating system.

BSP – board support package; information and drivers for a specific circuit board.

Buffer – a temporary holding location for data.

Bug – an error in a program or device.

Bus – data channel, communication pathway for data transfer.

Byte – ordered collection of 8 bits; values from 0-255

C – programming language from Bell Labs, circa 1972.

Cache – faster and smaller intermediate memory between the processor and main memory.

Cache coherency – process to keep the contents of multiple caches consistent,

CAN – controller area network.

CAS – column address strobe (in DRAM refreshing)

Chip – integrated circuit component.

Clock – periodic timing signal to control and synchronize operations.

CMOS – complementary metal oxide semiconductor; a technology using both positive and negative semiconductors to achieve low power operation.

Complement – in binary logic, the opposite state.

Compilation – software process to translate source code to assembly or machine code (or error codes).

Configware – equivalent of software for FPGA architectures; configuration information.

Control Flow – computer architecture involving directed flow through the program; data dependent paths are allowed.

COP – computer operating properly.

Coprocessor – another processor to supplement the operations of the main processor. Used for floating point, video, etc. Usually relies on the main processor for instruction fetch; and control.

Core – early non-volatile memory technology based on ferromagnetic torroid's.

Cots – commercial, off-the-shelf.

CPU – central processing unit.

D/A – digital to analog conversion.

DAC – digital to analog converter.

Daemon – in multitasking, a program that runs in the background.

Dalvik – the virtual machine in the Android operating system.

Dataflow – computer architecture where a changing value forces recalculation of dependent values.

Datagram – message on a packet switched network; the delivery, arrival time, and order of arrival are not guaranteed.

DDR – dual data rate (memory).

Deadlock – a situation in which two or more competing actions are each waiting for the other to finish, and thus neither ever does.

DCE – data communications equipment; interface to the network.

Denorm – in floating point representation, a non-zero number with a magnitude less than the smallest normal number.

Device driver – specific software to interface a peripheral to the operating system.

Digital – using discrete values for representation of states or numbers.

Dirty bit – used to signal that the contents of a cache have changed.

DMA - direct memory access (to/from memory, for I/O devices).

Double word – two words; if word = 8 bits, double word = 16 bits.

Dram – dynamic random access memory

DSP – digital signal processing.

DTE – data terminal equipment; communicates with the DCE to get to the network.

DVI – digital visual interface (for video).

EIA – Electronics Industry Association.

Embedded system – a computer systems with limited human interfaces and performing specific tasks. Usually part of a larger system.

Epitaxial – in semiconductors, have a crystalline overlayer with a well-defined orientation.

Eprom – erasable programmable read-only memory.

EEprom – electrically erasable read-only memory.

Ethernet – 1980's networking technology. IEEE 802.3.

Exception – interrupt due to internal events, such as overflow.

Fail-safe – a system designed to do no harm in the event of failure.

FET – field effect transistor.

Fetch/execute cycle – basic operating cycle of a computer; fetch the instruction, execute the instruction.

Firewire –serial communications protocol (IEEE-1394).

Firmware – code contained in a non-volatile memory.

Fixed point – computer numeric format with a fixed number of digits or bits, and a fixed radix point. Integers.

Flag – a binary indicator.

Flash memory – a type of non-volatile memory, similar to EEprom.

Flip-flop – a circuit with two stable states; ideal for binary.

Floating point – computer numeric format for real numbers; has significant digits and an exponent.

Forth – stack-oriented programming language

FPGA – field programmable gate array.

FPU – floating point unit, an ALU for floating point numbers.

Full duplex – communication in both directions simultaneously.

Gate – a circuit to implement a logic function; can have multiple inputs, but a single output.

Giga - 10^9 or 2^{30}

Gnu – recursive acronym; gnu (is) not unix. Operating system that is free software.

GPL – gnu public license used for free software; referred to as the "copyleft."

GPS – global processing system (U.S.) system of navigation satellites.

GPU – graphics processing unit. ALU for graphics data.

GUI – graphics user interface.

Half-duplex – communications in two directions, but not simultaneously.

Hall effect - production of a voltage across an electrical conductor, transverse to an electric current in the conductor and a magnetic field perpendicular to the current. Used in sensors.

Handshake – co-ordination mechanism.

Harvard architecture – memory storage scheme with separate instructions and data.

HDLC – high level data link control.

Hexadecimal – base 16 number representation.

Hexadecimal point – radix point that separates integer from fractional values of hexadecimal numbers.

HP – Hewlett-Packard Company. Instrumentation and computers.

Hypervisor – virtual machine manager. Can manage multiple operating systems.

Hysteresis – system dependency on current state and path (or history).

I2C – inter-integrated circuit; a multi-master serial single-ended computer bus invented by Philips.

IDE – Integrated development environment for software or configware.

IEEE – Institute of Electrical and Electronic Engineers. Professional organization and standards body.

IEEE-754 – standard for floating point representation and operations.

Infinity - the largest number that can be represented in the number system.

Integer – the natural numbers, zero, and the negatives of the natural numbers.

Interrupt – an asynchronous event to signal a need for attention (example: the phone rings).

Interrupt vector – entry in a table pointing to an interrupt service routine; indexed by interrupt number.

I/O – Input-output from the computer to external devices, or a user interface.

IP – intellectual property; also internet protocol.

IP core – IP describing a chip design that can be licensed to be used in an FPGA or ASIC.

IR – infrared, 1-400 terahertz. Perceived as heat.

ISA – instruction set architecture, the software description of the computer.

ISO – International Standards Organization.

ISR – interrupt service routine, a subroutine that handles a particular interrupt event.

Java – programming language that targets the Java Virtual Machine.

Jazelle – direct execution of Java bytecodes, as opposed to execution in the Java Virtual Machine.

Joystick – human interface device for rotation and direction control. Used in aircraft and video games.

JPEG – Joint Photographic Experts Group's standard for image compression.

JTAG – Joint Test Action Group; industry group that lead to IEEE 1149.1, Standard Test Access Port and Boundary-Scan Architecture.

Junction – in semiconductors, the boundary interface of the n-type and p-type material.

JVM – Java Virtual Machine – software that allows any architecture to execute Java bytecodes by emulation.

Kernel – main portion of the operating system. Interface between the applications and the hardware.

Kilo – a prefix for 10^3 or 2^{10}

LAN – local area network.

Latency – time delay.

LCD – liquid crystal display.

LED – light emitting diode.

LET – linear energy transfer. Used to characterize ionizing radiation.

GNU/linux – unix-like operating system developed by Linus Torvalds; open source.

LISP – programming language for list processing (1958).

List – a data structure.

Little-endian – data format with the least significant bit or byte at the highest address, or transmitted last.

Logic operation – generally, negate, AND, OR, XOR, and their inverses.

Logo – programming language for education and robotics, based on LISP (1967).

Loop-unrolling – optimization of a loop for speed at the cost of space.

LRU – least recently used; an algorithm for item replacement in a cache.

LSB – least significant bit or byte.

LUT – look up table.

Mac – media access control; a mac address is unique on a network.

Machine language – native code for a particular computer hardware.

Mainframe – a computer you can't lift.

Malware – malicious software; virus, worm, Trojan, spyware, adware, and such.

Mantissa – significant digits (as opposed to the exponent) of a floating point value.

Master-slave – control process with one element in charge. Master status may be exchanged among elements.

Math operation – generally, add, subtract, multiply, divide.

Mega - 10^6 or 2^{20}

Memory leak – when a program uses memory resources but does not return them, leading to a lack of available memory.

Memory scrubbing – detecting and correcting bit errors.

MEMS – Micro Electronic Mechanical System

Mesh – a highly connected network.

MESI – modified, exclusive, shared, invalid state of a cache coherency protocol.

Metaprogramming – programs that produce or modify other programs.

Microcode – hardware level data structures to translate machine instructions into sequences of circuit level operations.

Microcontroller – microprocessor with included memory and/or I/O.

Microkernel – operating system which is not monolithic. So functions execute in user space.

Microprocessor – a monolithic CPU on a chip.

Microprogramming – modifying the microcode.

MIL-STD-1553 – military standard (US) for a serial communications bus for avionics.

MIMD – multiple instruction, multiple data

Minicomputer – smaller than a mainframe, larger than a pc.

Minix – Unix-like operating system; free and open source.

MIPS – millions of instructions per second; sometimes used as a measure of throughput.

MOSI – modified, owned, shared, invalid cache coherency protocol

MMU – memory management unit; translates virtual to physical addresses.

Modem – modulator/demodulator; digital communications interface for analog channels.

MPEG – Motion Picture Experts Group (standard for compressing video).

MRAM – Magnetorestrictive random access memory. Non-volatile memory approach using magnetic storage elements and integrated circuit fabrication techniques.

MSB – most significant bit or byte.

MSI – modified, shared, invalid cache coherency protocol.

Multiplex – combining signals on a communication channel by sampling.

Mutex – a data structure and methodology for mutual exclusion.

Multicore – multiple processing cores on one substrate or chip; need not be identical.

NAN – not-a-number; invalid bit pattern.

NAND – negated (or inverse) AND function.

NASA – National Aeronautics and Space Administration.

NDA – non-disclosure agreement; legal agreement protecting IP.

Nibble – 4 bits, ½ byte.

NIST – National Institute of Standards and Technology (US), previously, National Bureau of Standards.

NMI – non-maskable interrupt; cannot be ignored by the software.

NOR – negated (or inverse) OR function

Normalized number – in the proper format for floating point representation.

NRE – non-recurring engineering; one-time costs for a project.

Null modem – acting as two modems, wired back to back. Artifact of the RS-232 standard.

NUMA – non-uniform memory access for multiprocessors; local and global memory access protocol.

NVM – non-volatile memory.

Nyquist rate – in communications, the minimum sampling rate, equal to twice the highest frequency in the signal.

OBD – On-Board diagnostics; for automobiles, a state-of-health systems for emissions control.

Octal – base 8 number.

Off-the-shelf – commercially available; not custom.

Opcode – part of a machine language instruction that specifies the operation to be performed.

Open source – methodology for hardware or software development with free distribution and access.

Operating system – software that controls the allocation of resources in a computer.

OSI – Open systems interconnect model for networking, from ISO.

Overflow - the result of an arithmetic operation exceeds the capacity of the destination.

Packet – a small container; a block of data on a network.

Paging – memory management technique using fixed size memory blocks.

Paradigm – a pattern or model

Paradigm shift – a change from one paradigm to another. Disruptive or evolutionary.

Parallel – multiple operations or communication proceeding simultaneously.

Parity – an error detecting mechanism involving an extra check bit in the word.

Pascal – a programming language (circa 1970).

Pc – personal computer, politically correct, program counter.

PCB – printed circuit board.

PCI – peripheral interconnect interface (bus).

PCIe – pci Express (next-gen pci)

PCM – pulse code modulation.

PDA – personal digital assistant; pocket-sized device; palmtop; 1984; superseded by functions in mobile phones.

Peta - 1015 or 250

Pic – a microcontroller from

Piezo – production of electricity by mechanical stress.

Pinout – mapping of signals to I/O pins of a device.

Pipeline – operations in serial, assembly-line fashion.

Pixel – picture element; smallest addressable element on a display or a sensor.

PLD– programmable logic device; generic gate-level part that can be programmed for a function.

Posix – portable operating system interface, IEEE standard.

PROM – programmable read-only memory.

PWM – pulse width modulation.

Python – programming language.

Quad word – four words. If word = 16 bits, quad word is 64 bits.

Quadrature encoder – an incremental rotary encoder providing rotational position information.

Queue – first in, first out data buffer structure; hardware of software.

Rad – unit of absorbed radiation dose; 100 ergs per gram; also, radian, angular measurement.

RAID – random array of inexpensive disks; using commodity disk drives to build large storage arrays.

Radix point – separates integer and fractional parts of a real number.

RAM – random access memory; any item can be access in the same time as any other.

RAS – Row address strobe, in dram refresh.

Register – temporary storage location for a data item.

Reset – signal and process that returns the hardware to a known, defined state.

RISC – reduced instruction set computer.

ROM – read only memory.

Router – networking component for packets.

Real-time – system that responds to events in a predictable, bounded time.

RS-232 – EIA telecommunications standard (1962), serial with handshake.

SAM – sequential access memory, like a magnetic tape.

SATA – serial ATA, a storage media interconnect.

Sandbox – an isolated and controlled environment to run untested or potentially malicious code.

Script – a program for an interpreter. Used to automate tasks.

SDRAM – synchronous dynamic random access memory.

Segmentation – dividing a network or memory into sections.

Self-modifying code – computer code that modifies itself as it run; hard to debug

Semiconductor – material with electrical characteristics between conductors and insulators; basis of current technology processor and memory devices.

Semaphore –signaling element among processes.

Sensor – a device that converts a physical observable quantity or event to a signal.

Serial – bit by bit.

Server – a computer running services on a network.

Servo – a control device with feedback.

Seu – single event upset; radiation induced upset in a device.

Shift – move one bit position to the left or right in a word.

Sign-magnitude – number representation with a specific sign bit.

Signed number – representation with a value and a numeric sign.

SIMD – single instruction, multiple data.

Simm – single in-line memory module.

SOC – system on chip

Software – set of instructions and data to tell a computer what to do.

SMP – symmetric multiprocessing.

Snoop – monitor packets in a network, or data in a cache

SRAM – static random access memory.

Stack – first in, last out data structure. Can be hardware of software.

Stack pointer – a reference pointer to the top of the stack.

State machine – model of sequential processes.

Superscalar – computer with instruction-level parallelism, by replication of resources.

SWD – serial wire debug.

Synchronous – using the same clock to coordinate operations.

System – a collection of interacting elements and relationships with a specific behavior.

System of Systems – a complex collection of systems with pooled resources.

Table – data structure. Can be multi-dimensional.

Tera - 10^{12} or 2^{40}

Test-and-set – coordination mechanism for multiple processes that allows reading to a location and writing it in a non-interruptible manner.

TCP/IP – transmission control protocol/internet protocol; layered set of protocols for networks.

Thread – smallest independent set of instructions managed by a multiprocessing operating system.

Thumb – a 16-bit instruction subset and operating mode for the ARM processor.

TLB – translation lookaside buffer – a cache of addresses.

TMR – Triple Modular Redundancy; an error control mechanism using redundant components.

Transceiver – receiver and transmitter in one box.

Transducer – a device that converts one form of energy to another (example: the Grand Coulee Dam).

Transputer – a microcomputer on a chip by Inmos Corp., circa 1980. Innovative communication mechanism using serial links.

TRAP – exception or fault handling mechanism in a computer; an operating system component.

Triplicate – using three copies (of hardware, software, messaging, power supplies, etc.). for redundancy and error control.

Truncate – discard. Cutoff, make shorter.

TTL – transistor-transistor logic in digital integrated circuits. (1963)

UART – universal asynchronous receiver-transmitter. Parallel-to-serial; serial-to parallel device with handshaking.

Ubuntu – Gnu-GNU/linux variant.

UDP – User datagram protocol; part of the Internet Protocol.

USART – universal synchronous (or) asynchronous receiver/transmitter.

Underflow – the result of an arithmetic operation is smaller than the smallest representable number.

UPS – uninterruptable power supply. Backup power source.

USAF – United States Air Force.

USB – universal serial bus.

Unsigned number – a number without a numeric sign.

Vector – single dimensional array of values.

VHDL- very high level description language; a language to describe integrated circuits and asic/ fpga's.

VIA – vertical conducting pathway through an insulating layer in a semiconductor.

Virtual memory – memory management technique using address translation.

Virtualization – creating a virtual resource from available physical resources.

Virus – malignant computer program.

Viterbi Decoder – a maximum likelihood decoder for data encoded with a Convolutional code for error control. Can be implemented in software or hardware

VLIW – very long instruction word – mechanism for parallelism.

Voip – voice over Internet Protocol.

VxWorks – real time operating system from WindRiver Corp.

Von Neumann – John, a computer pioneer and mathematician; realized that computer instructions are data.

Watchcat – watches the watchdog

Watchdog – hardware/software function to sanity check the hardware, software, and process; applies corrective action if a fault is detected; fail-safe mechanism.

Wiki – the Hawaiian word for "quick." Refers to a collaborative content website.

Word – a collection of bits of any size; does not have to be a power of two.

Write-back – cache organization where the data is not written to main memory until the cache location is needed for re-use.

Write-only – of no interest.

Write-through – all cache writes also go to memory.

X86 – Intel -16, -32, 64-bit ISA.

Xen – Hypervisor, U. Cambridge.

XOR – exclusive OR; either but not both.

Zener – voltage reference diode.

Zero address – architecture using implicit addressing, like a stack.

Bibliography

Computer Architecture, General

Bell, C. Gordon and Newell, Allen, *Computer Structures: Readings and Examples*, McGraw-Hill Inc., 1971, ISBN- 0070043574.

Blaauw, Gerrit A. and Brooks, Frederick P. Jr. *Computer Architecture, Concepts and Evolution*, 2 volumes, 1997, Addison-Wesley, IBN 0-201-10557-8.

Boole, George *An Investigation of the Laws of Thought on which are Founded the Mathematical Theories of Logic and Probability*, 1854, Reprinted 1958, Dover, ISBN 0-486-60028-9.

Bryant, Randal E. and O'Hallaron, David R. *Computer Systems: A Programmer's Perspective*, 2nd edition, Addison Wesley, Kindle e-book edition, ASIN: B004S81RXE.

Burks, Arthur; W. Goldstein, Herman H.; Von Neumann, John *Preliminary Discussion of the Logical Design of an Electronic Computing Instrument*, 1987, MIT Press, originally published in *Papers of John Von Neumann on Computing and Computer Theory*.

Carter, Nick Schaum's *Outline of Computer Architecture*, McGraw-Hill; 1st edition, 2001, ISBN- 007136207X.

Comer, Douglas E. *Essentials of Computer Architecture,* Prentice Hall, 2004, ISBN 0131491792.

Englander, Irv *The Architecture of Computer Hardware and Systems Software: An Information Technology Approach*, Wiley; 3rd edition, 2003, ISBN-0471073253.

Everett, R. R. and Swain, F. E. *Project Whirlwind, Report R-127, Whirlwind I Computer,* Servomechanisms Laboratory, M.I.T., Sept 4, 1947.

Harris, David and Harris, Sarah *Digital Design and Computer Architecture*, Morgan Kaufmann,, 2007, ISBN 0123704979.

Hennessy, John L. and Patterson, David A. *Computer Architecture, Fifth Edition: A Quantitative Approach*, Morgan Kaufmann,, 2011, ISBN 012383872X.

Heuring, Vincent, and Jordan, Harry F. *Computer Systems Design and Architecture*, Prentice Hall; 2nd edition, 2003, ISBN 0130484407.

Johnson, William M. *Superscalar Microprocessors Design*, Prentice Hall PTR; Facsimile edition, 1990, ISBN 0138756341.

Kidder, Tracy *The Soul of a New Machine*, Back Bay Books, 2000, ISBN 0316491977.

Mano, M. Morris *Computer System Architecture* (3rd Edition), Prentice Hall; 3rd edition, 1992, ISBN 0131755633.

Murdocca, Miles J. and Heuring, Vincent *Computer Architecture and Organization: An Integrated Approach*, Wiley, 2007, ISBN 0471733881.

Nisan, Noam and Schocken, Shimon, The Elements of Computing Systems: Building a Modern Computer from First Principles, 2005, MIT Press, ISBN 0262640686.

Null, Linda *The Essentials of Computer Organization and Architecture*, Jones & Bartlett Pub; 2 edition, 2006, ISBN 0763737690.

Page, Daniel, *A Practical Introduction to Computer Architecture*, 2009, Springer, ISBN 1848822553.

Patterson, David A and Hennessy, John L: *Computer Organization and Design: The Hardware/Software Interface*, Revised Fourth Edition, Morgan Kaufmann, 2011, ISBN 0123744938.

Patterson, David A and Hennessy, John L. Computer Organization and Design: The Hardware/Software Interface, ARM Edition, Morgan Kaufmann, 2011, ISBN 8131222748.

Ramachandran, Umakishore, and Leahy William D. Jr., *Computer Systems: An Integrated Approach to Architecture and Operating Systems*, 2010, Addison Wesley, ISBN 0321486137.

Reid, T. R. *The Chip: How Two Americans Invented the Microchip and Launched a Revolution,* Random House Trade Paperbacks; Revised edition, 2001, ISBN 0375758283.

Shriver, Bruce D. T*he Anatomy of a High-Performance Microprocessor: A Systems Perspective*, Wiley-IEEE Computer Society Press, 1998, ISBN 0818684003.

Silc, Jurji, Robic, Borut, Ungerer, Theo *Processor Architecture: From Dataflow to Superscalar and Beyond*, Springer; 1st edition, 1999, ISBN 3540647988.

Stakem, Patrick H. *A Practitioner's Guide to RISC Microprocessor Architecture*, Wiley-Interscience, 1996, ISBN 0471130184.

Stakem, Patrick H. *Computer Architecture & Programming of the Intel x86 Family*; 2012, PRB Publishing, ASIN: B0078Q39D4.

Stakem, Patrick H. *Architecture of Massively Parallel Microprocessor Systems,* PRB Publishing, 2011, ASIN: B004K1F172.

Stakem, Patrick H. *The Hardware and Software Architecture of the Transputer*, 2011, PRB Publishing, ASIN: B004OYTS1K.

Stakem, Patrick H. *Microprocessors in Space*, 2011, PRB Publishing, ASIN: B0057PFJQI.

Stakem, Patrick H. *Multicore Computer Architectures,* PRRB Publishing, 2nd ed, 2014, ASIN: B00KB2XIQ0.

Stakem, Patrick H. Computer *Virtualization and the Cloud,,* PRRB Publishing, 2013, ASIN B00BAFF0JA.

Stakem, Patrick H. *RISC Microprocessors, History and Overview* , PRRB Publishing, 2013, ASIN B00D5SCHQO .

Stallings, William *Computer Organization and Architecture: Designing for Performance* (7th Edition), Prentice Hall; 7 edition (July 21, 2005) ISBN 0131856448.

Stokes, Jon, *Inside the Machine An Illustrated Introduction to Microprocessors and Computer Architecture*, 2006, No Starch Press, ISBN 1593271042.

<<http://creativecommons.org/licenses/by-sa/3,0>> wikipedia, various. Material from Wikipedia (www.wikipedia.org) is used under the conditions of the Creative commons Attribution-ShareAlike #.0 Unported License.

Computer Arithmetic

Barrenechea, Mark J.; "Numeric Exception Handling", Programmer's Journal, May 1991, v 9 n 3 P 40.

Cavanagh, Joseph J. F. Digital Computer Arithmetic Design and Implementation, 1984, McGraw Hill, ISBN 0-07-010282-1.

Flores, Ivan *The Logic of Computer Arithmetic*, 1963, Prentice-Hall, ISBN 0135400392.

Hwang, Kai *Computer Arithmetic, Principles, Architecture, and Design*, Wiley, 1979, ISBN 0471034967.

Muller, Jean-Michel et al, *Handbook of Floating Point Arithmetic*, 2009, Birkhauser, ISBN 081764704X.

Muller, Jean-Michel *Elementary Functions: Algorithms and Implementation*, 2005, Birkhauser, ISBN 0817643729.

Overton, Michael L. *Numerical Computing with IEEE Floating Point Arithmetic*, Society for Industrial & Applied Math; 1st ed., April 2001, ISBN-978-0898714821.

Parker, "Am29027 Handbook", AMD, 1989.

Richards, R. K. *Arithmetic Operations in Digital Computers*, 1955, Van Nostrand, B00128Z00.

Rowen, Johnson, and Ries "The MIPS R3010 Floating Point Coprocessor", IEEE Micro, June 1988.

Schmid, Hermann *Decimal Computation*, 1974, Wiley, ISBN 0-471-76180-X.

Schwartzlander, E. and Lemonds, Carl (ed) *Computer Arithmetic a Complete Reference*, August 2012, Springer, ISBN 0387748830.

Scott, Norman R. *Computer Number Systems & Arithmetic*, 1984, Prentice-Hall, ISBN-0-13-164211-1.

Sterbenz, Patrick H. *Floating Point Computation*, 1974, Prentice Hall, ISBN 0133224953.

MC68881/882 Floating Point Coprocessor User's Manual, 1989, 2nd ed., Motorola, Prentice-Hall, ISBN 0-13-567009-8.

80387 Programmer's Reference Manual, 1987, Intel, 231917-001

32-bit Microprogrammable Products, Am29C300/29300 Data Book, 1988, AMD.

DSP96002 IEEE Floating-Point Dual Port Processor User's Manual, Motorola, DSP96002um/ad, 1989.

ANSI/IEEE Standard 754-1985 for Binary Floating-Point Arithmetic, IEEE Computer, Jan. 1980.

ARM Specific

Andrews, J. *Co-verification of Hardware and software for ARM SoC Design*, 1st edition, 2004, Newnes, ISBN 9780080476902, ASIN: B001464118.

Atheshian, Peter and Zulaica, Daniel *ARM Synthesizable Design with Actel FPGAs: With Mixed-Signal SOC Applications*, 2010, McGraw-Hill Professional, ISBN 0071622810.

Badawy, Wael and Jullien, Graham *System-on-chip for Real-time Applications*. 2003, Kluwer, ISBN 1-4020-7254-6.

Furber, Stephen B. *ARM System-on-Chip Architecture* (2nd Edition), 2000, Addison Wesley Professional, ISBN 9780201675191.

Furber, Stephen B. *ARM System Architecture*, 1996 Addison-Wesley, ISBN 0201403528.

Ghahroodi. Massoud M., Ozer, Emre, Bull, David *SEU and SET-tolerant ARM Cortex-R$ CPU for Space and Avionics Applications, www.median-project.eu/wp-content/.../median2013_submission_5.pdf*

Gibson, J. R. *ARM Assembly Language - an Introduction*, 2007, Lulu enterprises UK Ltd. ISBN 1847536964.

Hohl, William *ARM Assembly Language: Fundamentals and Techniques,* 2009, CRC Press, ISBN 1439806101.

Jagger, Dave *ARM Architecture Reference Manual*, 1997, Prentice Hall, ISBN 0137362994.

Lamie, Edward *Real-Time Embedded Multithreading Using ThreadX and ARM*, Newnes; 2nd edition, 2009, ISBN 1856176010.

Lindberg, Van, *Intellectual Property and Open Source, A Practical Guide to Protecting Code*, 2008, O'Reilly Media, ISBN 0596517963.

Mahout, Vincent *Assembly Language Programming: ARM Cortex-M3*, Wiley-ISTE; 1st edition, March 6, 2012, ISBN-10: 1848213298.

Nicholson, J. *Starting Embedded GNU/linux Development on an ARM Architecture,* 1st ed., Newnes, Jul 2013, ISBN 9780080982366.

Patterson, David A and Hennessy, John L. *Computer Organization and Design: The Hardware/Software Interface*, ARM Edition, Morgan Kaufmann, 2011, ISBN 8131222748.

Predko, Michael *Programming and Customizing the ARM7 Microcontroller*, 2011, McGraw-Hill/Tab, ISBN 0071597573.

Seal, David ARM *Architecture Reference Manual,* 2nd Edition, 2001 Addison Wesley, ISBN 0201737191.

Sloss, Andrew; Symes, Dominic; and Wright, Chris *ARM System Developer's Guide: Designing and Optimizing System Software*, Morgan Kaufmann Series in Computer Architecture and Design, 2004, ISBN 9781558608740.

St. Laurent, Andrew M. *Understanding Open Source and Free Software Licensing*, 2004, O'Reilly, ISBN- 0596005814.

Valvano, Jonathan W. *Embedded Systems: Introduction to the ARM Cortex-M3*, CreateSpace Independent Publishing Platform, May 26, 2012, ISBN 1477508996.

Valvano, Jonathan W. *Embedded systems: Real time Interfacing to the ARM Cortex-M3,*
CreateSpace Independent Publishing Platform, 2010, ISBN-10: 1463590156.

Valvano, Jonathan W. *Embedded systems: Real-Time Operating systems for the ARM Cortex-M3,* CreateSpace Independent Publishing Platform, January 3, 2012, ISBN-10: 1466468866.

Van Someren, Alex and Atack, Carol, *ARM RISC Chip: A Programmer's Guide*, 1994 Addison Wesley, ISBN 0201624109.

Yiu, Joseph *The Definitive Guide to the ARM Cortex-M0*; 2nd Edition; 2011, Newnes; ISBN 978-0123854773.

Yiu, Joseph *The Definitive Guide to the ARM Cortex-M3*, 2nd Edition, 2009, Newnes, ISBN 185617963X.

*Acorn Risc Machine Data Manua*l, VLSI Technology, 1990, Prentice Hall, ISBN 0-13-781618-9.

VL86C010, 32-bit RISC Microprocessor, VLSI Technology.

ARM600 data booklet. VLSI, June 1992.

VL86C010 32 bit RISC CPU and Peripherals User's Manual, VLSI Technologies, Inc., 1989, Prentice-Hall, ISBN 0-13-944968-X.

ARM Product family, ARM60 Microprocessor, GEC Plessey, March, 1993, Pub. DS3553.

ARM Product family, ARM610 Microprocessor, GEC Plessey, March, 1993, Pub. DS3554.

3rd Generation Intel XScale(R) Microarchitecture Developer's Manual, http://www.intel.com/design/intelxscale/316283.htm

ARM Papers, a selection

Boyd-Merrit, Rick and Clark,; Peter "Intel to reveal details on StrongARM chip" EE Times, 24 July 1998.

Cantrell, Tom "More Than a Core," Silicon Update, Circuit Cellar, Issue 213, April 2008, www.circuitcellar.com.

Case, Brian "ARM-600 Targets Low Power Applications," Brian Case, Microprocessor Report, Vol. 5, No. 23, Dec 18, 1991.

Case, Brian "ARM Architecture Offers High Code Density," Microprocessor Report, Vol. 5, No. 23, Dec 18, 1991.

Clarke, Peter, "Why the ARM architecture is shaped the way it is," EETimes, 11/26/2012.

Clements, Alan "ARMs for the Poor: Selecting a Processor for Teaching Computer Architecture," ASEE/IEEE Frontiers in Education Conference, Oct 27-30, 2010, Washington, DC.

Gandhi, Prashant P. "SA-1500: A 300 MHz RISC CPU with Attached Media Processor". Hot Chips 10, 18 August 1998.

Montanaro, James et al. (1997). "A 160-MHz, 32-b, 0.5-W CMOS RISC Microprocessor," Digital Technical Journal, vol. 9, no. 1. pp. 49–62.

Pountain, Dick "ARM600: RISC Goes OOP," BYTE, Dec, 1991.

Pountain, Dick "The Archimedes A310" product review, BYTE, Oct. 1987.

Pountain, Dick; "Under The Hood: A Call to ARM", BYTE, Nov 1992 v 17 n 12 p 293.

Stephany, R. et al. (1998). "A 200MHz 32b 0.5W CMOS RISC Microprocessor". ISSCC Digest of Technical Papers, pp. 238–239, 443.

Turley, Jim "Embedded Vendors Seek Differentiation". Microprocessor Report, pp. 16–21, 12 September 1996.

Turley, Jim. "Newton First Design Win for StrongARM". Microprocessor Report, p. 5, 18 November 1996.

Williams, Martyn "Intel puts StrongARM on death row". InfoWorld, Feb. 2003.

"Digital targets supercharged StrongARM chip at consumer electronics market" PR Newswire. 1996-02-05.

Digital Equipment Corporation "Digital Targets Supercharged StrongARM Chip At Consumer Electronics Market" Press release, Feb. 5, 1996.

Digital Equipment Corporation "Digital's StrongARM Chips Pull Away in Embedded Race". Press release, 12 September 1996
.
Intel Corporation "Intel Introduces StrongARM Products for PC Companions". Press Release, 7 October 1998.

Intel Corporation "Intel StrongARM Processor, Companion Chip Optimized For Handheld Computing Devices" Press release, 31 March 1999.

VLSI Technology VL86V010, An Affordable 32-bit RISC Microprocessor System.

STM32F103x8 Datasheet, STI, April 2011, Doc ID 13857 Rev 13.

Java Virtual Machine Specification, http:// java.sun.com/docs/books/vmspec/

Selected documents available from www.ARM.com:

Cortex-M3 Technical Reference Manual, 2006, ARM Ltd. ARM DDI 0337E.

ARMv6-M Architecture Reference Manual, 2010, ARM Ltd. ARM DDI 0419C.

ARM Architecture Reference Manual, 2005, ARM Ltd, ARM DDI 01001.

Cortex-A5 Specification Summary.

Cortex-A7 Specification Summary.

Cortex-A8 Specification Summary.

Cortex-A9 Specification Summary.

Cortex-A15 Specification Summary.

Cortex-R4 Specification Summary.

Cortex-R5 Specification Summary.

Cortex-R5 & Cortex-R7 Press Release January 31, 2011.

Cortex-R7 Specification Summary.

Cortex-M0 Specification Summary.

Cortex-M0 Instruction Set.

Cortex-M1 Specification Summary.

"ARM Extends Cortex Family with First Processor Optimized for FPGA", ARM press release, March 19, 2007.

Cortex-M3 Specification Summary.

Cortex-M4 Specification Summary.

If you enjoyed this book, you might find something else from the author interesting as well.

Stakem, Patrick H. *16-bit Microprocessors, History and Architecture*, 2013 PRRB Publishing, ASIN B00D5ETQ3U.

Stakem, Patrick H. *4- and 8-bit Microprocessors, Architecture and History*, 2013, PRRB Publishing, ASIN B00D5ZSKCC.

Stakem, Patrick H. *Apollo's Computers,* 2014, PRRB Publishing, ASIN B00LDT217.

Stakem, Patrick H. *The Architecture and Applications of the ARM Microprocessors,* 2013, PRRB Publishing, ASIN B00BAFF4OQ.

Stakem, Patrick H. *Earth Rovers: for Exploration and Environmental Monitoring,* 2014, PRRB Publishing, ASIN BOOMBKZCBE.

Stakem, Patrick H. *Embedded Computer Systems, Volume 1, Introduction and Architecture*, 2013, PRRB Publishing, ASIN B00GB0W4GG.

Stakem, Patrick H. *The History of Spacecraft Computers from the V-2 to the Space Station*, 2013, PRRB Publishing, ASIN B004L626U6.

Stakem, Patrick H. *Floating Point Computation*, 2013, PRRB Publishing, ASIN B00D5E1S7W.

Stakem, Patrick H. Architecture of Massively Parallel Microprocessor Systems, 2011, PRRB Publishing, ASIN B004K1F172.

Stakem, Patrick H. *Multicore Computer Architecture,* 2014 , PRRB Publishing, ASIN B00KB2XIQD.

Stakem, Patrick H. *Personal Robots*, 2014, PRRB Publishing, ASIN BOOMBQ084K.

Stakem, Patrick H. *RISC Microprocessors, History and Overview,* 2013, PRRB Publishing, ASIN B00D5SCHQO.

Stakem, Patrick H. *Robots and Telerobots in Space Application*s, 2011, PRRB Publishing, ASIN B0057IMJRM.

Stakem, Patrick H. *The Saturn Rocket and the Pegasus Missions, 1965,* 2013, PRRB Publishing, ASIN B00BVA79ZW.

Stakem, Patrick H. *Microprocessors in Space*, 2011, PRRB Publishing, ASIN B0057PFJQI.

Stakem, Patrick H. Computer *Virtualization and the Cloud*, 2013, PRRB Publishing, ASIN B00BAFF0JA.

Stakem, Patrick H. *What's the Worst That Could Happen? Bad Assumptions, Ignorance, Failures and Screw-ups in Engineering Projects, 2014,* PRRB Publishing, ASIN B00J7SH540.

Stakem, Patrick H. *Computer Architecture & Programming of the Intel x86 Family, 2013,* PRRB Publishing, ASIN B0078Q39D4.

Stakem, Patrick H. *The Hardware and Software Architecture of the Transputer*, 2011,PRRB Publishing, ASIN B004OYTS1K.

Stakem, Patrick H. *Mainframes, Computing on Big Iron*, 2015, PRRB Publishing, ASIN B00TXQQ3FI

Stakem, Patrick H. *Spacecraft Control Center*, 2015, PRRB Publishing, ASIN tbd. Due 2016.

Stakem, Patrick H. *Embedded in Space,* 2015, PRRB Publishing, ASIN-B018BAYCCM

Stakem, Patrick H. *Extreme Environment Embedded Systems*, PRRB Publishing, ASIN tbd. Due 2016

Stakem, Patrick H. *A Practitioner's Guide to RISC Microprocessor Architecture*, Wiley Interscience, 1996, ISBN 0471130184.